Sunglasses 25cents

A Gypsy-Minded Soul

SUZIE MORWOOD

BALBOA.PRESS
A DIVISION OF HAY HOUSE

Balboa Press books may be ordered through booksellers or by contacting:

Balboa Press
A Division of Hay House
1663 Liberty Drive
Bloomington, IN 47403
www.balboapress.com
844-682-1282

Print information available on the last page.

ISBN: 978-1-9822-6864-0 (sc)
ISBN: 978-1-9822-6865-7 (e)

Balboa Press rev. date: 05/11/2021

A Gypsy Soul

They make fortunes come true.

Do not get on a gypsy's bad side.

Why are they so bad?

Their clothing is colorful

Huge tents protect them

She wears sparkly beaded long scarves.

Chunky jewellery

Henna-stained hands

Resourceful, free spirited,

Mysterious, very majestic, traditional…

Like Dorothy on a yellow brick road

She hopes her ruby shoes get up there quick

She left everyone she loves at home.

Contents

A Gypsy-Minded Soul

A Gypsy-Minded Soul

CHAPTER ONE

This is My Turn to Speak

This story is about me of course.

I wanted to have center stage for once, up front and in your face.

I was born into a lovely and potentially normal family. I had four parents unlike some people. My mom and dad … and then there were my grandparents who were very protective of me and thought the sun rose and set for me. That is l how the cliché goes.

I was an only child for seven years and 5/6 months. Then my world totally changed. I had wanted a sibling because everyone I went to school with had one and all my neighbourhood chums had a sibling. It was great pretending for awhile that I had a big brother that would defend me and no one knew he was a tiny baby in a crib.

We got along until he was about 5 years old. That may be a stretch but there were a few moments through the years as well, and the dear Lord knows, that I have tried to get along with him but maybe not enough. There is a great age difference but he was very protected from all harms way.

I had a great life and my parents were wonderful to me, and I never wanted for anything. I never asked for anything but then again, I was a little shy about asking for anything. That did change a little over the years though.

My mom was my encourager, my dad too, but I spent way more time with my mom because my dad was a travelling salesman most of my growing up years until I was about 15, most of my growing up years. Mom always wanted me to be a nurse. I never really thought about it one way or another. My parents were in charge and I never questioned much until years and years later. I had a dream when I was in high school of becoming a teacher, but my mom always wanted me to become a nurse. Now, I think that she had always dreamed of nursing for herself but she didn't complete high school.

She had wanted to go to work and make her own money. Her father ran a grocery store in Prince Albert, Saskatchewan and she loved working in the store as well. She never did get paid for doing that. So, when she was old enough, she quit high school, went to secretarial school, and got a job at a place called Western Grocers as their secretary.

Then there was my dad. He quite often would joke that he only went to grade 2, but I knew well enough that that was not true. I learned so much about him when my mom passed away. He used to tell us about going to St. Anne's School in Digby, Nova Scotia It was a Catholic private school for boys. He still speaks quite favorably about this place, and he has for years. I used to think it was a place for bad boys but found out later it was for spoiled boys. He was the youngest of three and the only boy and they always gave him special treatment. When I say special, I mean because he was a boy. He did not used to believe that, but we have had conversations about this over the years and he finally did agree with me. One for me. Lol.

He later went to The University of King's College, in Halifax, Nova Scotia, which was established in 1789. It is the oldest chartered university in Canada, and the first English-speaking university in the Commonwealth outside the United Kingdom. He did not complete the program. Instead, he became a salesman, the job he absolutely loved. He still, to this day, says that it was his dream job. He loved to talk to people and be the center of attention. Well, at least the focal point in a conversation. He always has had so much to say. He was, and is, very well read. He always used to have a book going. When I look back over the years, now even more since he has gotten up in years, I realize that he mostly just reads his prayer book or his Bible.

This brings me to Kings' College again. My dad and two other friends went there as adult students to get degrees in Theology. They were all working and married at the time. Dad and his friend Charley Moulton did not complete their Theology Degree, which had been their intention, and so they could not become ordained priests. Family life was in the way. The third member of the trio did complete his degree, and he was ordained. He was a little more unique in the fact that he did not have any children and his only responsibility was his wife and himself so he could focus on his goal. This was Ted Burton.

CHAPTER TWO

Camping with the Church Family

1958

You should know before you go any further in my story that later in my career, I became known as Gypsy Sue because my lifestyle suited the nickname.

How I remember Ted Burton is that he was a lovely man who was known from his work at St. Phillips, our church in Halifax. Ted was older than Charlie Moulton or my dad, and he did not have children. Ted collected empty pop bottles along the roadside to pay for his classes. Well, by Gypsy Sue's standards, he seemed ancient because I was only nine years old at this point in the story.

Now we all know that Mommas always tells the truth, but I thought "no way". I had to ask my mother several times if Ted Burton's bottle collecting was in fact true, and each time she said that it was. She said that she had sometimes seen him collecting bottles but just thought he was being a good citizen, not knowing he was collecting the bottles to pay for his education. His wife was a sweet lady who did not work outside the home after 1956. She had been a schoolteacher, but women in those days did not usually work after they were married, so Ted was the sole wage earner which made it necessary for him to do the theological program part time. He used the pennies from bottle collecting to make his dream come true. He followed his dream or his calling. I never understood what that phrase meant, only that following your heart's desire was important, but Ted always said he was following a message from his Higher Power. Some people find that hard to believe. I can relate. I had always wanted to become a teacher but did not follow through and became a nurse. I had a great career but it was not my calling.

Now this action of Ted's seemed preposterous! A grown man collecting empty bottles to pay for his courses to become a minister. But not so outrageous when you knew his wife Marian. She was as thrifty as they come. They lived in a nice older house near us but the word meagre would have described their home … not poor, just the bare essentials. One thing I remember about Marion is she would sometimes have her sweater on inside out. "Well," she told me, "this is the way I found it and it will be the right side out the next time".

Ted Burton worked for the Nova Scotia Light and Power as a maintenance man before starting his studies. Yes! He really did collect pop bottles to help him pay for his books.

I always thought I was a shy kid but I guess selling sunglasses each summer was the way I broke the ice. Well, I am quite sure that this was what made me so flexible in later years.

1956

I started out as an only child and seven years and 5/6 months later it all changed. I am not too regretful but that fact has framed my life in many ways. The gypsy mindedness that is. Always doing something to keep the ball spinning in motion.

My brother was always a bundle of energy from the get-go. As the years went by, he had no problem telling others that I was his 'much older' sister. It is what it is. He made a lot of people laugh and was therefore very entertaining. I did have to watch him and look out for him though since he was so much younger. This was good training for when I would babysit and later on in life when I had my own children.

1965

I distinctly remember a time when I was left to look after him. Well supervise him more than anything. Mom and Dad had gone out and it was a Saturday evening when I was not going to be working at my part time job. He was being his usual irritating self. He went into my bedroom, took something precious of mine and then played the game of *"I got something of yours…"*. So, I decided to chase him around the house. We lived in one of those houses where there was a back hall that allows you circle the house. I started to chase him. By reaching forward, and grabbing him, I finally caught him and he fell partly on the kitchen stove. Well, nothing noticeable happened at that time, but some years later, his front tooth became dark and he had to have dental work. He would never let me forget that. These are just the things that happen with siblings.

1967

Then another time when my dad was away… It was my brother's birthday and my parents' anniversary. Just my mother and brother and I were there. My mother had made a birthday cake for the three of us. The candles were lit, and we were all ready to sing Happy Birthday to Colin when the phone rang. It was our father, and he was calling to wish everyone well, especially my mother since it was their anniversary too.

I must remind you that the candles were already lit so my brother thought he should blow them out but when he did this, the flames from the candles set fire to the table cloth and the table. My mother screamed and she hung up the phone. We were all in panic mode, and screaming at this point. Thankfully we put out the fire I have no idea what happened next, except Colin ran into his bedroom and we did not have cake. Years later, he told his now-wife that my mother and I had beaten him within an inch of his life. This never happened. The event was quite traumatic at the time and we survived the ordeal, but I am sure it has been imprinted in Colin's mind for years.

The topic of brain imprinting is spoken of in the book by Bessel van der Kolk called The Body Keeps Score.

CHAPTER THREE

My Very First Job

My very first job was minding Colin, my younger brother and only brother, but there was no money in that.

1958

My first real paying job came when I was about 10 years old. It was selling sunglasses to all my family's friends when we went camping on the July long weekend. Every summer, five families from our church went camping. For several years, we camped at The Ovens, located just a stone's throw from the mouth of Lunenburg Bay. This was in the late 50's and thousands of visitors would walk the spectacular trails along the cliffs to view the famous sea caves, or as we knew them, The Ovens. Many were day-visitors, but we went as overnight guests on the July 1st long weekend about three years running. Each family had two children, so there was always someone to hang out with but most were boys, except for the McBrides, and they had three girls. They were always a little snobby toward everyone else, or so it seemed. The McDonalds had Harry and Brian, and most of the girls had a crush on Harry … but he did not have time for anyone. He was so much older than everyone else. So, we diverted our attention to Brian.

Other years we went to the campgrounds in Louisburg which is in Cape Breton.

Lunenburg is a port town on the South Shore of Nova Scotia, Canada. Founded in 1753, the town was one of the first British attempts to settle Protestants in Nova Scotia.

The economy was traditionally based on the offshore fishery and today Lunenburg is the site of Canada's largest secondary fish-processing plant. The town flourished in the late 1800s, and much of the historic architecture dates from that period.

In 1995 UNESCO designated it a World Heritage Site. UNESCO considers the site the best example of planned British colonial settlement in North America as it retains the original layout and appearance of the 1800s, including local wooden vernacular architecture. UNESCO considers the town in need of protection because the future of its traditional economic underpinnings, the Atlantic fishery, is now very uncertain.

The historic core of the town is also a National Historic site of Canada.

Louisbourg is also well known as the site of the Fortress of Louisbourg. The original settlement appeared in the later 1500s, and was initially called Havre à l'Anglois, or English Harbour. Subsequently, a fishing port grew up there to become a major commercial port and in 1713 a strongly defended fortress was built there by the French. The fortifications eventually surrounded the town. The walls were constructed mainly between 1720 and 1740. By the mid-1740s, Louisbourg, named for Louis XIV of France, was one of the most extensive (and expensive) European fortifications constructed in North America. It was supported by two smaller garrisons on Île Royale (Cape Breton) located at present-day St. Peter's and Englishtown. The Fortress of Louisbourg had two key weaknesses: it was erected on

low-lying ground overlooked by nearby hills and its design focused attention mainly toward sea-based assaults, leaving the land-facing defences relatively weak. A third weakness was that it was a long way from France or Québec, from which reinforcements could be sent. It was captured by British colonists in 1745 and was a major bargaining chip in the negotiations leading to the 1748 Treaty of Aix-La-Chappelle which ended the European War of the Austrian Succession. It was returned to the French in exchange for border towns in what is today Belgium. It was, however, captured again in 1758 by British forces in the Seven Years' War and its fortifications were systematically destroyed by British engineers.[2] The British continued to maintain a garrison at Louisbourg until 1768.

The fortress and the town were partially reconstructed in the 1960s and 1970s as a living history museum. The project stands as the largest reconstruction project in North America and provided jobs for unemployed Cape Breton coal miners. The head stonemason for this project was Ron Bovaird and the site is operated by Parks Canada. (Wikipedia)

1958

Now back to my first paying job. Halifax is where I was born and grew up for the first 15 years of my life.

I had seen an advertisement in a comic book offering me a chance to make some real cash by selling fashionable plastic sunglasses for 25 cents, and I answered it. I do not remember if I asked my mother for permission or not, but I must have since I had to send a money order. Before I knew it, there was the mailman at the front door with a little cardboard box.

I came by this trade very honestly; my dear ole' dad was a salesman for over 30 years and as the old saying goes he could sell refrigerators to the people of the north. And here is another saying that applies, "The apple didn't fall very far from the tree".

In many ways I am more like my dad than my mom but I do have the quiet and reserved nature of my mom. I was always one who did not question anything as a child or even as an adult, but as I got up in years, I did change my ways and eventually was prepared to disagree with my dad on many issues. I have become a little more outspoken over the years because my career has involved dealing with people in crisis, and I needed to become quite a strong person for that. I am so very much like my dad. He sold the Star Weekly as a kid. He always liked to tell about how the paper cost 10 cents and he made 2 cents per paper. Now that may be about as far as the similarities go with being like my dad. Unlike my dad, I did not carry on the lifestyle of a salesperson. My brother also sold and delivered the Star Weekly, but he jammed out many times and I had to deliver it for him because my mother told me to do it.

Dad always had a car allowance and an expense account. (I had to create that for myself.) He travelled considerably with his job as well, and he usually was away Monday to Friday for three weeks a month, so my mother was the main disciplinarian. We spent a lot of time at #7 Mic Mac Street, which is where my grandparents lived. We lived at the bottom. It was # 72 Mic Mac Street the house with vertical red siding.

Summer camping was great! It was so much fun asking everyone in the campsite if they wanted a pair of plastic sunglasses for only 25 cents. Mrs. Burton, Ted's wife, was the first person to buy a pair and she also bought a pair the next summer when I was selling them again. I even got up enough courage to go to neighbouring campsites and ask other people to purchase sunglasses. Before I knew it, the box was empty and I had to order another selection of sunglasses.

I made some money, not a lot, but enough for a ten-year-old, and I was saving it to go shopping in Bangor, Maine, in August to buy my school clothes. This shopping trip was also an annual event. Today, I hear my granddaughter, Icey, trying to think of ways she can make money. There does not seem to be an avenue for young children to start out like that today. I do not know if there are even any comic book ads offering sunglasses for sale. I should look. Icey wants to make money to save for a career in broadcasting. Well, she needs $1,000 to get started. That would be lots of sunglass at 25 cents each. Since starting to write this story though, she has changed her focus and wants to go to Yale and get her Master's in Criminology.

My life, as I was growing up, revolved around our church, St. Philips Anglican. My mother was involved in the Altar Guild and the Women's Auxiliary. She and my grandmother were both always baking something for the church. My dad too was on the church council and had helped with the building of the church. So, it would follow that I too would be as involved. I was in the choir (still cannot carry a tune in a bucket). I was also in the Girls' Auxiliary and, of course, there was the Girl Guides too. They were not church related, but the groups met in the church.

I was involved in Guides, so I never had an opportunity to get into any trouble. We lived just across from the back door to the church, so we had no excuse for missing any meetings. I have one vivid memory of the time I went to the church on a Saturday afternoon to practice for a special choir performance, and it was an icy afternoon, very cold and windy. I left the choir practice by the side door, heading around the north side and towards our house. Well, I lost my footing and slipped on the ice, crashing down on my head. I saw stars! Of course, all the rest of the members of the choir had left in the other direction, so I was out there on my own. My head was numb. I staggered to the house, which was not far, but I do remember my head was sore and soft from the bang.

With sincere reflection of that day, it may have even been a mild concussion but I was not checked and it wasn't a big deal at the time. My momma greeted me at the door and got me to sit down, and then she applied ice immediately. She always knew what to do. She always would offer a remedy. I remember when my first daughter was born. Mom would change her diapers and if there was any sign of diaper rash, she thought you needed to apply burnt flour. Well, doesn't that sound weird? She would toast a little in the oven and then apply it. It seemed to work, and I trusted her.

1975

Dear ole Mom! I so miss her. Here is another little tidbit. If I left one of my daughters to be babysat by mom and I did not leave enough clean tops, she would just turn one inside out, and it would be all clean. Priceless antics.

So even if the roads were too bad, or we thought we were too far away to walk to get to an activity, it was never too far away for us to get to church. We had no excuse. Most of my friends were at the church. There was Barbara Coolen, and Margaret Cox, and there was Doreen Monroe and Darlene Smith. These last two friends didn't go to the church but they were my neighbours for the years I went to St. Andrews up until grade 6. This was the year that my family moved up to Connaught Avenue, right behind the minister's house.

2019

I finally reconnected with Doreen recently and she has remarried after her first husband passed away. He too was a friend of ours, and his family went to the same church. He was "that cute Jimmy Fletcher". I have some wonderful memories from that period of my life but they seem to have become less clear than the ones I formed when my family moved because of my father's job transfer. We used to play red light green light but no one does that any more. Instead, they are on their mobiles playing games such as "Words with Friends or Farm house or there is Candy Crush".

CHAPTER FOUR

Changing Schools

1960 s

When we moved to Connaught Ave, I had to change schools from St. Andrew's Elementary to Westmount Elementary. Mr. Crocket was the principal and a true character. He was probably shorter than me at the time, and since our family was all so tall, he seemed like a "little person" to me. He had such a funny little voice, but he was very stern with everyone. He taught the girls Health and Sex Education but there was nothing about the birds and the bees in it, so I am not sure why they called it Sex Education.

When I was in Grade 8, I remember being paged over the loudspeaker, "Susan Taylor. Please come to the office" (Taylor was my name before I married.) I did not know what it was about, so I headed directly there and was told my brother had run away from his class. He was in kindergarten at the time, so I had to go and find him. He could not follow the rules even back then. I headed home which was like half a block away. On my way through the minister's yard to take the short cut to our house, there he was between the two garages, hiding. He did not want to go back to school, so I took him home so mom could deal with this little monster who was always trying to get someone's attention. He never liked going to school or any kind of restrictions. This has not changed at all. Maybe he was a free spirit, we will never know. I cannot remember if there were consequences, but I just headed back to school. Looking back, I am sure there were likely no consequences. Through the years when he was doing something that would be ordinarily corrected, I would ask Mom why? She would always say, "Oh, it is just a phase he is going through".

CHAPTER FIVE

Becoming One of the Crowd

It was in 1963 that the Beatles where popular and I was in Grade 9 at the time at Westmount school. I was always taller than everyone. I always felt like the giant amongst my friends. We moved to a different school district and the transition was difficult at first, especially losing all my old friends. I had a nice life and I have no major complaints about my life.

There was a group of girls at his new school who always seemed to parade around like they were better than everyone else. They wore cool clothes, and everyone else was dirt, so they seemed to think. That is how you sometimes see it when you are 14 years old. These girls were what we would classify as bullies today. I was not bullied though. I remember that year distinctly and I recall purchasing 45 rpm records with the hits of the BEATLES. I had quite a collection and it included some of the tunes that the cool girls could not get, so I was one up on them. And for some reason, they wanted me to be part of their group. I hung around with them a little at school but I was always too involved with other things, like the youth group at our church, girl guides and choir practice.

1962

My love interest at the time was Robert Peacock. He was everyone's heart throb and he did take me to the show once. It had to be a show because I was so much taller than he was, and the difference was not all that noticeable sitting down in a movie theatre. That connection did not last long. He was from a different neighbourhood. We were upper middle class, not upper class but not lower class either. My mother was very conscious of this difference for sure. You do not fraternize with those from the "other side of the track".

"The other side of the track" refers to a part of the town that is particularly impoverished and, therefore, undesirable. The word "track" refers to railroad tracks, and often is thought of as demarcating different economic areas of town. Sometimes the families who lived "on the wrong side of the tracks" had immigrated from other parts of the world and worked at low paying jobs, Other families were single parent families, something that in the late fifties and early sixties was never talked about.

I do recall that Robert was quite cute and very slim, and he did have a bit of a swagger to his stroll. A lot of the girls had a crush on Robert too! But he was a wild thing for sure. Once again, I dodged a bullet. But the expression "dodge a bullet" doesn't specifically mean you escape from being shot. Instead, it is used more generally to mean avoiding any situation that turns out to be disastrous.

1963

I think the big highlight of Grade 8 and 9 for me were the Home Economics classes which were held at the little school house across the road from our church. It was there that we learned to cook and sew. I really enjoyed this. At the end of each year, there was a fashion show that featured the garments we had created.

My grandfather on my mother's side was a professional tailor, and he sewed clothes for all of us, so he was especially impressed by my work. The dress I made that year, I remember, had turned out rather well. I do recall it was made of a flower print that now I would consider to be a granny print. I do not think I ever wore it in public again after the fashion show. Some of the things I learned to cook I still make and I use the same techniques. Those lessons have stayed with me all these years. I am a grandmother now and still can remember the lemon loaf with the lemon juice that drizzled all the way through the cake. Mmmmm … good! We made fruit cake too, and I used to make them for Christmas gifts, baking them in little empty cans from fruits or veggies and sending them to relatives.

CHAPTER SIX

The Beginning of High School

1964

In September of 1964, I started Grade 10 at Queen Elizabeth High school in Halifax and had a full load of courses: all three sciences, French, English and math. All was going well until October. Then my Dad was transferred to Saint John, New Brunswick, with his job. I was just getting used to taking the city bus to school, walking home with all the cool kids, and getting fully engrossed in the subjects at high school. The song that rings in my head when I remember that time is a Roy Orbison's "Pretty Woman". I wasn't too thrilled about the move but I smiled and nodded and didn't make much fuss. That was always what I did.

I was initially sad because I had just started high school and had to leave all my friends behind. All I can recall about the move was that it happened fast. There was a going-away party for my parents, but that was it. It was like we were transported from Halifax to Saint John in one quick swoop, just like they did on Star Wars with Captain Kirk and his gang. Luckily, I did make friends fast. This was most important part to me, so I guess I was not as shy as I thought. It seemed like we now lived worlds apart, so far away when you have not done any travelling. I did see one or two of my friends when I visited my grandmother in Halifax, and a few times my new friend in Saint John and I flew to Halifax to visit them. That was quite an exciting thing. Two 16-year-old girls alone on an airplane. Whoa…we still remember those trips.

1964

Gypsy Sue is on the road again.

This was the beginning of my moving about from province to province and that part of my life is a distant memory… but good things always come out of life changes. I can hardly remember Halifax, except I know it was good times We lived in a grand house, I had my own room, I always had new clothes, and I never had to wear hand-me-downs. I was the oldest and they usually do not wear hand-me-downs. It was the same for my brother, who was, and still is, 7 years and 10 months younger than me. He never had to wear hand-me-downs either. We did wear a lot of clothes that were tailor-made by my grandfather, the professional tailor. He made me a new suit every Easter, a pleated skirt and jacket, and my brother would get a new pair of trousers when he was small. He did get a few suits of short pants and jackets. He used to be so adorably cute. He has been headstrong and a force to reckon with all his life.

I remember one traumatic experience when he put his arm through the ringer washer. We still to this day have no idea how he got free or even how he got his body up so high to put his arm through the wringer part.

1964

When we first got to Saint John, we were living in a motel called the Fundy Motel right on Manawagonish Road. It was still there on our last visit just a few years ago. There was quite a view from our motel room over what is know as the Golden

Mile, a mile-long stretch comprised of many businesses. That was where my Dad's office was located, right in the middle of all the car dealerships as well as many factories. My Dad's company was called Pilkington Glass and it originated in St. Helens, England, but it no longer exists by this name as it was sold to a Japanese company after he retired.

He loved to tell his story, one of many, about how he got the job. He always says my mother got him the job. She had sent in a letter of interest along with a resume, and I presume, that he got a call. "If it wasn't for your mother, I would never have got the job." I sometimes wonder if he is putting himself down or building up my mother's prowess. I am thinking it is the latter since he loved her so much. After she passed, he could not stop thinking about her. He would sit and stare all day at her picture. Well after 72 years of being together. Whoa…nobody stays married that long. Many people do not live that long.

My parents had already decided on a place for us to live when we moved to St. John, but it was not available quite yet and our furniture and all our precious belongings had not arrived. We were all in this big motel room together. I do not think we were there more than one or maybe two nights before our furniture arrived. Dad had to take me to school the second day and the after that I was on my own.

I can still remember my dear sweet momma laying on her bed in her room sobbing and wishing she lived back in Halifax. She missed being close to her parents. She had never lived this far away from them except for the year when she was in Grade 7 and travelled by train from Prince Albert, Saskatchewan, to Shelburne, Nova Scotia. She and her parents were awfully close. I didn't quite know what to say to my mom when she was feeling sad but we muddled through the loneliness and got our house in order. I used to come home after school on the city bus and help mom sort through the boxes until I got the house in order.

The house was very nice and it bordered on a wildlife refuge area so we had a lot of racoons and other animals paying us a visit from time to time. Our garage was a little different. It was at the back of the house and so we didn't really use it for the car. Many nights we would neglect to close the garage door and when I went downstairs with the garbage, I would find some empty food cans, licked clean and shiny. Then one night I went down with the garbage and saw what I thought was a raccoon…but it turned out it was a skunk I let out this blood curdling scream. I then put the lights on and he ran away. It is a good thing the skunk left or he might have sprayed me with his "Eau de Skunk".

My Dad used the garage to sell used antique furniture, so it was always full. He had a friend, Mr. Clark on PEI, who was his contact person. My parents were always wheeling and dealing, and Mom loved to go to garage sales. She had lots of her own as well.

The part of Saint John where we lived was called Lancaster. We, who lived there, liked to differentiate between West Saint John and Lancaster. I was a little bit of a snob sometimes when it suited me.

Our house was in the old part of Lancaster which has now been incorporated into Saint John West. My brother was to go to Barnhill School and I was to go to Saint John High. That meant that I had to ride over the bridge on the city bus everyday, which was fine. It was too far to walk. The distance from my house on Hillcrest Drive to downtown Saint john was about 9 miles. It was a bit of a ride but the scenery was great. I did have to be up and gone early to catch the bus by 7.30 am otherwise I would be late. If we missed the bus, we were hooped. My mother couldn't drive as yet and neither could I and we only had one car at this time.

The worst part of the journey was the return home trip in winter. If I missed the last bus in the evening, I would have to walk across a field which was in front of an orphanage. Manawagonish Road overlooked the Golden Mile so it was barren and open to blustery winds. If I were early enough coming home, I could stop off at the top of the hill by my Dad's office and get a ride home with him. That did not happen very often though. Many times, I would just get off at my friend Marla's house with her and I would call Dad to pick me up on his way home. Sometimes I would study while I was waiting, but mostly Marla and I would just hang out or else she would be working on a sewing project.

CHAPTER SEVEN

Our Move to Saint John

My initial recollection of Saint John, apart from the Fundy Motel, which by the way is still there, was driving up to my new school. Saint John High was noticeably big and incredibly old, marble stairs led up to the front door and we-my parents and I- went into the Principal's Office. His name was Mr. Ward and he was a giant of a man. He wore thick rimmed glasses, had a brush-cut hairstyle, and wore a grey serge suit. His greeting was stern and his reception was gruff. There was no time spent on ceremony. I was quickly enrolled in Grade 10 and placed in my home room with Mr. Louis. He was also my French teacher. My parents left me and headed out to take my little brother to his new school. Only then did I realized that I would have to make my way home on the city bus. Previously, I could either walk home or take the bus, something I hardly ever did. I found this quite a transition, but I coped and made new friends. For the most part, everyone at this new school was quite friendly as far as I remember. Of course, there were the cool kids but I never was part of this group there. Well, I guess you could say that I was part of my own cool group.

The journey home on the bus took at least an hour since there were so many stops and we lived almost at the end of the line. On the way home one day, I think it was the second day, I met my life long best friend, Marla. I think it was probably my first day on the bus going home that I met Marla. She asked me if I wanted to go bowling with her and another friend, Marsha, on Friday night. I, of course, never did turn down anything like this. It was the beginning of a lifelong connection and a deep friendship. We have remained friends to this very day, even though thousands of miles have separated us, from Canada's east coast to its west coast. Marla has always said that she is shy and introverted, but on this day she proved otherwise. I went home with her and met her mother who was wonderful.

2005

My dear ole Dad loves to tell the story of one time in 2005 when we were visiting Marla in her home. We were chitchatting away in the kitchen and Dad said to Albert, Marla's husband, "What is it with those two? They just pick up where they left off." Albert replied, "I have no idea." and then rolled his eyes with his friendly smirk. We did, however, end up following totally different paths. We did marry within a month of each other but Marla never left Saint John. She had four kids and I had two. This was one of my greatest regrets that Frank and I didn't have more children, but it is too late now. Cannot live with regrets. Although I also know that if I had stayed there, the events of my life would have been totally different. I would not have met my husband and had my two beautiful daughters.

Marla and I did a lot together, and her parents and her home became my second home. Please do not think my home life was horrible; in fact, it was quite the opposite. Mom was always there since she did not work outside the home. She had a nice life and was highly active in her own life with us and the church, The Church of the Good Shepherd Anglican in Lancaster. She did not drive, as I already mentioned, but she became good friends with the Reids, our neighbours across the street. Fran did drive so they went a lot of places together. Dad was the sole provider and we always lived in a nice house with a yard in a good neighbourhood. I have a lot to be thankful for.

There were so many years that my brother and I did get along. He was a royal pain but everyone thought he was cute. And he was cute. We just had nothing in common. This was his downfall. My mom was often on her own because my Dad travelled so much. she was often so overwhelmed with her little boy. He was treated somewhat like a prince. "Don't hurt him!", "Now Susan, you need to be an example to your little brother.", "Look after him,", "It is just a phase." she would say. I never could quite get my head around it, so I would just stay away and go to Marla's house after school. In all honesty, these phrases continued until he was well in his teens. It probably made it easier for my mother if I were not there as there would be no hassling and no fighting. I am sure there was a fight every night at the dinner table. Maybe not a fight, just a tussle. He was always a challenge to me, or so it seemed. No word of exaggeration! But my Dad always says, "but he is my son". I just don't believe the nonsense that goes with 'My Son'." Children are children and we all need to have discipline and boundaries. Everyone needs a picket fence to rein them in and keep order.

Marla's house was my escape from our home where my little brother was always causing havoc. I have no idea how my mother made it to 91. She never knew what to say to him, and she always seemed to be afraid of him. I am sure it was very frustrating too. I know I avoided mostly since. I tried to wake him up for school one morning on instructions from my mom, and he swung his arm across his body and it belted me. I don't think it was necessarily just meant for me but I was there and he didn't want to get out of bed.

2009

I recall years later, in fact about 10 years ago, before my mom passed away... and believe me she was bright as can be right up until her last breath. She and I were sorting out her papers and receipt.

We were chatting about life and family and this and that. We always had these little times together when we would solve all the world's problems in an afternoon. We chatted about all her neighbours and their kids. She was always curious about how we were all doing. She had a wicked sense of humor. There was always twinkle in he r eye and you just knew she was going to crack a joke.

That's is when my dad would pop in the room with my brother and they would wonder with great curiosity what we were talking about. We of course couldn't tell them what was going on in to our curious minds.

CHAPTER EIGHT

Meeting My New Best Friends

1966-1969

I usually would get off the bus several stops before Hillcrest Dr. and my Dad would pick me up on his way home. It was more fun to stop over at Marla's house than take the bus all the way home and must entertain Colin, if I went home I had to help with supper which I didn't mind at all. But the ideal situation was to stay at Marla's and do more sewing. . This is when I perfected my sewing skills.

Marla taught me how to sew a dress in an afternoon. She was always sewing something so she figured she should teach me too. When Dad came to pick me up, he would just drive right into Marla's backyard and I would run out the door. I had a great set up. Thank you, Dad, for all you did, you are the best, and Mom too.

I had a date with someone on my dance card, think it was Bobby Marlow,sadly he has passed away now,, and I had to have a new dress. I wish I still had that dress! Well, it would never fit around me now. It was navy blue with sunflowers all over it. Marla also taught me how to make a lined pair of slacks and how to match the plaid perfectly.

I used to go with Marla and her family to their summer and winter retreat at Dipper Harbour. If her parents did not stay down at the harbour house for the weekend, then Gina, Marla's older sister, would also be dropped off, along with all the supplies. Gina was our chaperone. She was extremely strict too. Very unforgiving as well. So strict with us girls.

There was not much to do down there but walk the roads and visit the friends we knew. Some of these were friends and some were Marla's cousins who lived in Dipper Harbour or Mace's Bay. Some of them were bussed into Saint John High and some were bussed to St. Malachy's Boys High School. Marla's cousin, Grant Jones, lived in the Harbour. He was Marlene Donnelly's boyfriend at the time. I think she carried a torch for him for an awfully long time. That is just my take. There was a guy named Sammy Williams and I had a crush on him, perhaps because he was such a rebel. He had quit school after Grade 9, and he was a biker. He had a Harley Davison. Nice guy but not someone my family would be impressed with for me. I do not know where he lived in Dipper Harbour. He was a loner but everyone in Dipper Harbour loved Sammy, leathers and all. When we went down there, he and I would hang out, but I do not think I was ever on his bike. He was a little rough around the edges and a bit scruffy too. Not sure why I was attracted to this boy/man. He may have been charming, but I am not sure what the attraction was. Maybe it was because I was not home, and I was free to do what I pleased. To me he was an older man but he was a high school drop out, so he seemed older. Poor Sammy has passed away too.

Marla's neighbour at the Dipper Harbour, Greg Thompson, was a classmate from St. John High. He was so quiet and always seemed embarrassed and red-faced. I also had a crush on him too. His family were fishermen and quite successful. Greg was supposed to become a doctor, but I am not sure if he ever did. I think he continued in the family fishing business.

There was a dance party at Marla's place and all the boys from Dipper Harbour showed up. Marla had also invited a few handsome fellows who we all were sweet on as well, but I don't think she was really all that sweet on anyone down there. She just enjoyed going to Dipper. We still reminisce about our times at Dipper. Marlene and I reminisced more. Marla doesn't go there anymore and the house now belongs to her sister, Gina, and she doesn't let many people go there without her. Several years ago, my parents and I wanted to go to Dipper Harbour and perhaps stay in the house on our own. That was not going to happen; Gina had to be there. So, we changed our plans and went back to Saint John and stayed another night at Marla's place. Eventually we went on to get our flight to Bangor. We liked Gina but she was a little too controlling and liked to talk our ears off. Everyone felt the same way. She is a solitary soul. She is married but rides her husband too. Poor Albert, another Albert. (Marla also married an Albert)

When I was 16 years old, I figured I had to have a job. I just had the urge to have my own money, so I could buy my own clothes. I never really thought I should be asking my parents for money. The "sad" thing was my mother got the children's' allowance of $20 a month and gave this to me, so I really had lots of cash.

Does anyone remember when the family allowance came into existence?

Well, I will tell you now. The family allowance was Canada's first universal social program. It was rolled out 1945 as WWII was winding down and was intended to keep children from dying and to help stimulate the post war economy. The Family Allowance cheques would be mailed to the mothers of the households monthly, and they were non-taxable. Initially, mothers received from $5 to $13 depending on the age of the child. Every child received the same amount, based on the philosophy that every Canadian child was worthy of support. By the 1960s, it had risen to $20

Some people objected, claiming the allowance was a waste of taxpayer money since it would be distributed to the rich and poor alike while others saw this "baby bonus" as an attempt to lure votes, especially those voters with large families living in Quebec.

The reason I called my mother's actions "sad" were because, knowing what I know now, had I started saving my family allowance from the beginning, I would likely have been able to retire at age 55 instead of when I did. I no longer live in the world of "Should or could or would" I live in the world of "IS". I could have invested all that cash. Wow, the prospects are endless. Hindsight is 50/,50 that is for sure. A wise friend of mine said once, "We can't live in the "what ifs". Life isn't like that".

2016

"You can't go back". I am not sure that that is totally true but for the most part, yes, it is good to move on. It is never too late to start saving your money for a rainy day. Another dear friend who used to work at the Jordan Care Home tells of one of the residents used to repeat herself a lot and would say to my friend over and over, "You can't go back!!" So, we have coined that phrase now. I am not sure that is totally true. We moved back to New Brunswick after more than 40 years. We see my old high school friends but have made a new circle of wonderful friends and enjoy the lifestyle in the East Coast.

Now that we only have monthly pensions, my pension would be quite a lot more if I had not taken a lump sum out when my husband was having financial difficulties. As a result, I had to start from scratch again. We take out a set amount out of the bank right off the top before we start our monthly spending, and then we have money for a rainy day. A few times already, we have been able to save enough for a trip to Spain. So, it is worth the effort and so important to take that set amount right off the top before you start paying your bills; otherwise, it will be "gone like dinner".

CHAPTER NINE

Spending My Allowance

1966

My mother's family allowance of $20.00 a month. It should have been enough for me.

But nope, I had to apply for a job at Dominion Stores, a big Canadian grocery chain.

Dominion was a national chain of supermarkets in Canada, known as the Dominion of Canada when the chain was founded. The chain was founded in 1919 in Ontario and was later acquired by the Angus Corporation. It was later sold to The Great Atlantic & Pacific Tea company (A&P), which restricted the chain to the Greater Toronto Area. Stores outside Ontario were converted to the A&P banner or sold to third parties. A&P's Canadian division was later acquired by Metro Inc., which rebranded the remaining Dominion stores to its namesake banner in 2008. The store was founded by American businessmen Robert Jackson of New Hampshire and William J. Pentland of Connecticut. Pentland was manager of A&P stores in Connecticut and was hired by Jackson. By the end of 1919, they had a 20-store chain of which 18 were acquired from rival Loblaws. A year later, they had 61 stores. In 1929, Dominion tried to acquire a stake in Loblaws, but the stock market crash ended the

growth. During the Depression, Dominion lost both founders: Jackson went bankrupt and Pentland was killed in an auto accident in 1933.

Dominion's leadership was not resolved until 1939, when J. William Horsey became president. He in turn sold Dominion Stores to Angus Corporation. Smaller stores were consolidated from 574 to 195 by 1954. In the 1950s, Dominion began to build large stores with airy ceilings and large glass fronts. The chain also expanded beyond Toronto to other parts of Ontario, Quebec, Alberta, Manitoba, Saskatchewan, and Atlantic Canada. (Source: Wikipedia)

I was a grocery packer at Dominion for about a year and then I got hired on as a cashier. The starting wage for packers was 80 cents an hour. When I moved up to cashier, I got 95 cents an hour. Wowie!! Things were looking up. I worked most Friday and Saturday nights, so I would head right to work after school on Fridays. The thing was I had lots of money at my disposal, so now I could eat out for lunch every day and still have money to spare. I did not like making my own lunch and I did not particularly like homemade lunches either. It was not that the food was bad food, just that eating a sandwich was not very appealing. I usually ate at the Public Market in Saint John, which was a short walk from the high school. My besties and I would walk there right as the bell rang for lunch. Although it was a good walk to get to the uptown area, most of the students headed there for lunch in those days. Then, of course, there were those who had their own cars and would spend the lunch hour driving around the square, King's Square, that is. That is what all the cool guys did. At least they thought they were cool.

Saint *John* *is a seaport city on the Atlantic Ocean located near the mouth of the Bay of Fundy in New Brunswick, Canada. It is the oldest incorporated city in Canada, established by royal charter on May 18, 1785, during the reign of King George III. The port is Canada's third largest port by tonnage with a cargo base that includes dry and liquid bulk, break bulk, containers, and cruise ships.*

In the 2016 census, the city fell to second place, with a population of 67,575 over an area of 315.82 km² Greater Saint John_covers a land area of 3,362.95 km² or (1,298.44 sq mi) across the Caledonia Highlands, with a growing population of 126,202 (as of 2016).

Mi"maqand and Wolastoqiyik peoples lived in the region for thousands of years and called the river Wolastoq. French colonist, Samuel de Champlain, landed at Saint John Harbour in June 1604 (the feast of St. John the Baptist) and this is how the Saint John River got its name. The Saint John area was an important area for trade and defence for Acadia during the French colonial era and Fort La Tour, the city's harbour, was a pivotal battleground during the Acadian Civil War.

Saint John is the largest city in New Brunswick and the second largest city in the Maritime Provinces.

1969

I had made lots of friends while I worked at the grocery store. All the girls who worked part time there went to St. Vincent's Girls' Catholic High School, and the boys went to St. Malachy's. Oh, there was one girl, who went to St. John Vocational High School. It is strange that no one from the Saint John High school worked part time, at least none that I knew of. I probably should not have either; maybe I would have done better in school. Some St. John High students looked down their noses at the students who went to St. John Vocational, saying they were not as smart as those who went to the other high schools. We all knew that was not the truth, but there will always be those who see themselves as superior to others. It is everywhere, even today. It must just be the nature of some humans and it often comes out when we feel less than others ourselves, so we tend to put others down. It is the cruelty of humans as well.

1966

After work on either Friday night or Saturday night, we would all pile into someone's car or just walk up the hill to Reid's Diner which was on the corner opposite the Simms Brush factory and the Kimberley Clark paper towel factory. Those days always remind me of "Happy Days" the weekly TV show from years ago with The Fonz and Richie Cunningham and Al, who owned a diner. The Saint John's kids also used to go to the diner owned by a man named Al. I have this vivid imagination for sure. We would all go for milkshakes and chatter about all our gripes with the earth and Dominion Stores.

1966

My most terrifying memory of going to Reid's was the night I had access to my mother's car, an older blue Chrysler Valiant. I think it was a '63 which wasn't all that old then because it was 1966. It was a cool car and it had push button gears on the right side of the dash. Well, that was not the terrifying part. It happened while we were in the diner. We were laughing and telling stories, so I never noticed anyone leaving for a few minutes and then returning. When it came time to go, I went out to the parking lot and my mother's car was gone. Yes, it was gone. Oh my gosh, what would I do? What I did not know, was that while I was in the diner, a few of the guys had taken my mom's car and pushed it back down a fairly steep incline all the way to the grocery store parking lot.

Oh, I was so relieved that it was just a prank. The guys were so playful, just having fun but at my expense. It was so long ago now that all I remember is how glad I was to have retrieved my mom's car. I do not think I ever told my mom, probably best I did not. I did tell her most things though. She worried way too much, but then she probably knew more than I realize. I do know that I knew more than my girls realized I did sometimes.

2020

My mom always lived her life vicariously through me. I am sure I did a lot of things she wished she had done. She always encouraged me to go to school and get my education, so I did. I studied to become a nurse, a psychiatric nurse. When I was about to retire, she thought I was too young to do so. She said, "Stay working until you are 70." She wanted me to complete my Master's, so I did that, and then, I did my Doctorate as well, so she was able to see all that happen before she passed away. I sometimes wonder why I did all this studying. Was it for me, or for her? In the end, I know it was for both of us.

I do remember an infatuation that I had while working at Dominion Store. Well, a few actually! But this one was the most remarkable. I think he was my first love. His name was Jimmy, and he was very tall and very handsome. He looked like what I imagine my, now and of course my only, husband looked like when he was a young teenager. We kind of clicked, and we started to have a very mild romance after work, and at work we both would blush when we came into each other's space. On the way home from the diner, we were in the back seat of Ralph's 49 Ford When we stopped at our house, he leaned in and kissed me good night…and at that very moment, my Dad or it may have been my mother, started to flick the back-door light. It was so embarrassing, and I had to quickly get out of the car before he flicked that light too many times. The kisses were short but sweet.

1968

This infatuation, as I will call it, did not last too long. I told my mother that he was a Roman Catholic, but I am sure she already knew that since he went to the Catholic boy's high school. In those days, Protestants were not to get mixed up with Catholics, and she did not think my friendship with Jimmy was a good idea. I never saw any difference at all. The only thing I remember was that they ate fish on Fridays and had to go to confession. I was so curious that I even went to confession with my friends, Lise, and Suzanne Rose, who lived across the street from us on Micmac Street in Halifax. I didn't go into the box or cubicle with them, but I did sit at the back of the church. My mother thought strongly that I should not fraternize too much with Jimmy, so I cut it off with out any explanation. That was very weird on my part, but what could I say, "I can't go out with you anymore because you are Catholic?" Plus, I had no idea what to say. I still loved him or I thought so anyways.

Another time Ralph and Harvey, two other boys, drove me and Aida back to my place. My parents were out of town, travelling across the country by train to Prince Albert, Saskatchewan. I did not want to go; it would be no fun with my brother there. I was only 17 years old and although I was left alone to take care of the house, I had to sleep across the street at Katherine and Stewart Hazlett's house

The four of us teens had a fun time playing music and laughing and dancing in our front room. During the evening, Ralph and I made our way to the lower level of our house where there was a storage cupboard that was very dark. We both went inside, and we did a little canoodling but then I withdrew a bit and I remember to this day him saying, "Don't worry, you won't get pregnant". I was a little dumfounded by the statement and nervously laughed. Why would he say that? Guys say the darndest things to embarrass us females.

By then, it was quite late, after midnight, so I told them they had to go since I was sleeping across the street with our good neighbours. I thought they had very innocently just left and gone home, but in the morning when I returned to my house, I discovered that Ralph and Harvey had taken our extra house key off the top of the fridge and gone back into the house after I went to the Hazlett's. They had taken the bouquet of bull rushes that was in a vase in the living room and laid them out on the carpet and jumped all over them. It was an amazing mess. I was shocked and could not believe they had done this. So, my mission was to quickly clean it up and make it beautiful again before my mother returned. I was going to have a little difficulty finding more bulrushes to replace the damaged ones. When I went to work that night, Ralph and Harvey were looking a little smug and one of them, I do not recall which one, handed me my house key. We remained friends even after the fiasco. Boys will be boys…and they were a couple of pranksters. They were so likeable. No crush on either of them, just nice guys. We remained friends.

CHAPTER TEN

After School Jobs

1966

I cannot remember why I left the Dominion Stores chain, but I ended my job there and went to work in the cafeteria of the now defunct K-Mart.

*Kmart began as S.S. Kresge Corporation which then launched the **Kmart** chain in the U.S. in 1962 and soon expanded into **Canada**. Canada's Hudson's Bay Company purchased Kmart's 112 **Canadian** stores in 1998, closing some and converting others into Zellers. It leapt from the middle of the pack to being even bigger than Wal-Mart! Today, there is only one Zeller's store in Canada.*
(Source: Britannica)

I probably did not really have to work but I always wanted to have extra money to spend and I never wanted to ask Mom or Dad for money. Plus, I was such a social butterfly that I knew I would miss my circle of friends at work and I did not want to be home on Friday or Saturdays after school either. That K-Mart cafeteria job did not last too long. It was a horrible job. I mostly just washed the dishes and pots. Maybe that is why I hate doing dishes to this very day. There were the pots and pans that were dirty from the scallop potatoes and lasagna; the food was baked on hard as glass. I did not like the ugly outfit I had to wear, a yellow rayon skirt and blouse with a frilly white apron. I absolutely detested this job so I chose to quit and find another job. If I had to clean pots, they were going to be either my mother's pots or my own when I had my own place. I have never enjoyed kitchen work even when I had my own home. I did it because you cannot survive with a mess. Lucky my own girls were good at helping around the house. Now in later years, my husband loves to clean up after dinner or any meal. I consider myself incredibly lucky indeed.

1967

My dear father mentioned to a friend of his, Mr. Roydon Horncastle, that his daughter was looking for a weekend job and he just happen to be able to accommodate me. Mr. Horncastle had many business interests and dry cleaning was one of them. He was, well, just picture him. He was about 6" 4" tall and quite overweight, not fat just an exceptionally large man and he wore a lovely tweed overcoat and a beautiful top hat. He came in to see me in the store periodically and would sit on the customer side of the counter and chat. He was so dapper, such a handsome gentleman. Mr. Horncastle was the Bees Knees.

The "bee's knees" you say, "What is that?" It is one of several nonsense catchphrases that originated in North America in the 1920s, the period of the flappers. Nearly all the expressions from that era compared something of excellent quality to a part of an animal. You might have heard such curious concoctions as cat's meow, elephant's adenoids, bullfrog's beard, gnat's elbows, monkey's eyebrows, cat's whiskers, and dozens of others. Only a very few of these have survived in modern English, and bee's knees is perhaps the best known, though cat's pyjamas (an exception to the anatomical rule) also survives.

It was every Friday evening and all-day Saturday at a dry cleaner in the city, uptown near Kings' Square. All the action was on Friday nights, but the sidewalks were rolled up on Saturday nights. It was quiet and dull for night life in the city.

Today, it is little different, maybe even more exaggerate because so many businesses have closed in downtown Saint John. It is like a ghost street. We were just there two years ago for my 50th high school reunion and it has really gone down hill since I left. It looks dreadful. All the old shops are gone: MRA's (Manchester Robertson Allison's), Scoville's, and Calps' These stores had great stuff, fine linens, lovely clothes, and so much more. I really miss MRA's with the old-style elevators with the sliding grates. If you were looking for exercise, you could climb the old worn stairs to the top. So sad to see the negative progress in the city of Saint John. Now there is a mall with escalators to the top floor but sadly most of the shops are all empty there too. The rent is too high.

1968

Probably the most memorable thing about Kings' s Square when I worked at Dominion Stores was the crush, I had on a boy named Ralph, who went to the Catholic boy's school. He had a 1949 two-door maroon Ford and at noon hour, he would gather up some of his friends from school and drive around the Square downtown. This is the same Ralph who trampled bull rushes all over my mother's moss green carpet and I had a crush on him now. He was very funny. Never did see him again after high school and, of course, I left the province. I have since located him on Facebook.

I loved the job at the dry cleaners, got to do my homework, and work at the same time. Arvilla was the sweet lady who worked there fulltime. She lived uptown in an older flat in Saint John with her husband who was much older than she was. He didn't have much of a pension so her job was very important to them as they depended on the income. She was extremely sweet to me and had worked for Mr. Horncastle for many years.

I knew that for me, this job was just for extra cash until I got out of high school and moved onto higher education. My plans were to go into nursing although in my heart of hearts I did want to go to Teacher's College. I grew up thinking my parents were right and they would not steer me wrong about going into nursing. But I guess I felt my parents knew something I did not know so I did not question the fact that I did not really want to go to nursing school. I rarely questioned my parents' authority or decisions until later in life and only then in a kind way, of course. I vowed to encourage my own girls to walk their own walk and if that meant leaving home or going abroad to do the kind of things, they wished I was totally supportive.t. I have always believed that they should follow their dreams and become their own person. I wish I had been encouraged to do so. You can't go back!

Just a note here…maybe they took me too seriously as now one lives in India and one lives in Spain. I am just saying, "Be careful what you encourage."

Another benefit of my downtown job at the dry cleaners was that I was permitted to take my mother's car to work on Saturday, so I did not have to make my way home on the bus in the dark. A few times I did not go straight home. I went instead to East Saint John to see a love interest who will remain unnamed . He was a few years older and I met him through a co worker and, a friend at Dominion Stores. It was a big deal to have a potential boyfriend who was in university. He did not always have access to a car so I would go there, and we would watch television until quite late. Then I would head back home. It was a long way for a young girl to travel on her own. That love interest was a lost cause. Note what follows.

There was a time when Marla and I planned a wonderful dinner party at my place and Ian was my date and Marla had invited her boyfirend. to come over too. Well, on the afternoon of the party, my potential love interest called and cancelled. What an absolute jerk thing to do. What an absolute creep! I was really devasted, but we had to move on with the evening. So, there I was, scrambling to find a replacement. Thankfully, Marla called her Cousin Johnny, and he came in love interest's place. I never bothered with him again. We had a lovely evening.

CHAPTER ELEVEN

I Am A Social Butterfly

1968

This was the year I was supposed to graduate from high school and I was in Grade 12 for the first time. Most of my friends did graduate this year so it was no fun being left behind. I still consider Saint John High to be my school. This is where I spent my high school years and all my peeps were here. So, when there is a reunion this is where my loyalty goes but I hadn't played the game or followed the rules.

Instead, I played the fool and had way too much fun. Skipping classes and working every weekend meant that I spent a lot of time away from home. Don't get me wrong, my home life was fine and we lived in a very nice home in a good part of town. My parents were lovely, kind, generous and loving to a fault but I was always expected to see that my brother was not out of control and to be there when he was. He was a liability when it came to my life, as a teenager that is for sure. I was never quite sure how to handle the situations He was a little out of control. There are rules that applied to him. He had no chores to do. There was always so much conflict and noise. My Dad was away a lot and that may have had a bearing on his lack of discipline. Oh I guess boys will be boys.

Mom was raised an only child, and so she did not have any experience with children. She did have cousins that she saw regularly but since she worked in her father's grocery store, she really had no experience looking after children. The problem was he was the spoiled. He was not to be touched or corrected at least by his sister.

Unfortunately, I was too much of a social butterfly, worked too much, did not apply myself to my studies, and was faced with repeating Grade 12. My brother perpetually made a noise and I couldn't take the heat. I know I did study a lot with the radio on just to drown out his opposition to, slamming of doors and pacing about the house. He had a few friends and one of them lived across the street. Robbie Reid was a little tyrant as well, but he had the good sense to listen to his parents most of the time.

I did have difficulty focusing at home. I would always study with the radio playing rock music. So, my escape route was working at Dominion Stores and staying at Marla's place were only two of the ways of avoiding going home. When those did not cut it, there was always skipping school with a love interest and my involvement in the youth group at the Good Shepherd Anglican Church. I probably could have gone to Teachers College in Fredericton, but I had not graduated, and it was really important to me to finish things. I only needed enough points to go to teacher's college and I did have that. It still is important for me to complete what I start.

I knew I had to graduate so I made the decision to go to St. Vincent's Girls High School, a Catholic school. It was not that I had a lot of boy interests. Well, there was one, and my connection with him was probably one of my major distractions. This male friend did not get enough points to graduate either, but he was able to get into New Brunswick Technical School and took a two-year program to be an engineering technician. This is the same person I had a major crush on when I was in Grade 12 the first time. I was smitten big time and so was he, but he had a girlfriend he had been with for a few years. I had even been to his family's cottage. I met his brothers.

I was even stalked by a friend of his girlfriend to see what he had been up to since they had broken up.

We used to skip school together, and I am sure this contributed to my not getting the classes necessary to pass Grade 12. We parted ways at the end of that year when he decided he should go back to his old girl friend. He called me in late August to tell me his plans for the fall of 1968. and I told him my plans were to go to St. Vincent's to make sure I graduated. In hindsight I wished I had gone to teachers' college. We did not see each other again for many years.

I had a great time as always at St. Vincent's, made more friends, enjoyed the school, and did manage to pass all my courses, Yahoo! the nuns were very strict and were good at keeping us focused. The one course I did not participate in was Catechism, as I was of the Protestant persuasion. While the other girls were learning about the Catholic Church and its doctrines, I was in a study hall which made it possible for me to do my homework, something I might not have done when I got home.

I have not kept in touch with the girls from St. Vincent's as much as I have the ones from Saint John High. I still consider Saint John High as "my high school". I have never gone to the reunions at St. Vincent's. St. Vincent's has been demolished and the students, both girls and boys, all go to St. Malachy's High School the former boys' school.

The interesting part about the teachers at St. Vincent's was that they were members of the Sisters of Charity and wore religious habits. The habits, I remember were the shortened versions that fell just below the knees and were no longer the traditional black but rather teals, and blues, and browns. The sisters looked quite attractive.

The principal came marching into our classroom on the first day and danced around the class in her new habit. Sister Burns, I still remember her even though it was fifty years ago, has probably passed away by now. She was a short petite red-faced nun with her hair pulled straight back off her face. The nuns were very pleasant but expected us to tow the line. They were definitely strict! One nun in particular sticks in my mind and that was Sister Marcoux. She was my math teacher, a quiet woman who seemed old at the time.

Graduation was achieved and I applied to nursing as I had planned.

I was accepted into St. John General Hospital's School of Nursing. It was quite a thing to get accepted but I still, after all these years, wish I had gone to Teachers' College. I only lasted at the hospital for about three months and was asked to leave. It was a case of "I should have", but I was having so much fun once again and did not apply myself. Instead of Gypsy Sue, maybe I should have been called "Funtime".

Years, when I went to Nursing School in British Columbia, I did a practicum at St. Vincent's' Hospital in Vancouver and one of the sisters was a Sister of Charity. She was Sister Marcoux from St. Vincent's High School in Saint John. She was elderly but was in the convent in Vancouver for her retirement years, I think. A little too much like the twilight zone for my liking. She did remember me and said she was doing visitations at this hospital. It was not all that many years later, well about 14 years, so, I must have left an impression for sure. I was married and had two children before I decided to go back to school to become a nurse as certification in nursing only took three years and not the four, I would have needed to become a teacher.

1969

After graduation from St. Vincent's High School for Girls, I worked at Neilson's Clearing House where all the coupons and contests from all over North America were organized and counted. There were a lot of coupons and papers everywhere. This may well have been where I learned to get organized.

Neilson's Clearing House *was the brainchild of Chicago businessman Arthur C. Nielsen, Jr. It began Operations as a Nielson's Coupon Clearing House in 1957. With the growing volume of coupons being redeemed by consumers in the 1950's, Nielsen recognized the need for a clearing agent to help manufacturers and retailers manage the coupon reimbursement process more efficiently. So, a division was opened in Saint John New Brunswick.*

I travelled to work with Dot Murray, a neighbour and close friend of my mother's who worked their full time. She loved her work and was enormously proud of her job. I love it when people take pride in their work, whatever it is. She would do her knitting in the back of the car while Howard and I sat in the front seat for the journey to work. She loved her job. There is no shame in any job. We are all cogs in the wheel of life.

It was a busy job and paid well for the summertime. I was on a list to go to Nursing School at the Saint John General. Although I had enough points to get into the Teaching Program in Fredericton, my family thought it would be better to go to nursing. One of my great regrets is that I did not go to Teacher's College and follow my calling. It is important to follow your dream and not just live in the dreams. I needed to speak up and let people know my desire. This was, perhaps, my biggest fault in life I failed to do so many times in my career. I let other people step up and get ahead, or at least, take a leadership role.

Years later I was working on the psychiatric unit in Moncton Hospital and a patient on the unit who was in my care was walking about the unit quite arrogantly and had a definite presence about him. He was big and could be scary to some because of his large stature. I had a good nurse/patient working relationship and asked him, "How are you doing today?" I will never forget his response. "Oh Susan, I am living the dream." It didn't seem to be much of a dream to me but he did have 3 square meals a day, a roof over his head, and the run of the unit. He played the game somewhat; he was a border line personality and had a psychotic disorder.

***Borderline personality** is marked by an ongoing pattern of varying moods and behavior. These symptoms often result in impulsive actions and problems in relationships, intense episodes of anger, depression, and anxiety. The episodes can last for days. He did fit this criterion, but living the dream was an interesting response.*

1969

My mother and grandmother were thrilled to be going to the tea put on to celebrate the entry of a new group of students into the nursing program. There was a lot of prestige and hoopla attached as well. I did them proud for awhile.

The first night that the newbies were in residence was a nightmare, but fun and truly crazy. But it was a fun nightmare which is a contradiction. We had brought our trunks and clothes and moved into our respective rooms, and there was a great ruckus up and down the halls. I had been given a private room which was great, not sure why, but it was fantastic. While I was carousing up the halls, laughing and singing. the second year and third year students ransacked our rooms, and they spread our clothes everywhere. My trunk was dismantled into a right hot mess. So, I just closed my door and put it all back together. There was no point in making a scene because it would just be worse the next day when they would do it again, I thought. When I look back, I think it was quite funny. I would have also enjoyed being in on all that fun the following year as a second-year student. I think I have a little bit of a prankster in me. I just love to have fun. I still do. I must be laughing and having a good time.

2010

Oh, here I go digressing again, along the prankster storyline. But years later when I had retired and moved to Moncton, NB, a great friend and I decided to get dressed up for Hallowe'en and go treat or treating, but only go to the homes of people we knew. Well, we dressed so good that no one knew us until we hit the last house, one of her sisters-in-law. It wasn't that my friend was recognizable but she laughed her unique laugh and her sister-in-law said in a wee small voice as we were tripping done the stairs, "Isn't that you, Anne?" We just kept walking and laughing our guts out. Remember now at this point, we were in our 60's. We did have so much fun. Now that is about 8 years ago and I am so hoping that she will want to do that again. That probably will not happen for a while since 2020 was the year of the pandemic and Hallowe'en was more or less cancelled. The year 2020 was and is a life changer for the entire world.

Back to the story. There was one night that I decide to have a shower and took all my necessary belongings to the shower room, got into the shower and was happily foaming myself. Then it became insanely quiet. While I was in there some girls in the dorm decided to play a joke on me and took all my clothes and left me nothing but my birthday suit. It would have been okay to dash back to my room, but the floor matron just happened to come around to check everyone and chased me back to my room. That was so embarrassing, but hilarious too. I have always tried to see the funny side of everything because otherwise you will have so much baggage. "Just let it go" is one of my basic beliefs. Some would also add "Let go and let God". I never knew who had done this prank. but just as well. Embarrassing as it was running down the long hallway to my room, it was very funny.

On Wednesday nights, an exceptionally large group of the first-year nurses would gather in Pam Prince's room to watch Tom Jones on TV. She was the only one who had a television at our end of the dorm. What every happened to Pam Prince?

Do you know who Tom Jones is? *I can still hear him singing "It's not unusual to be in love with anyone". He is a Welsh singer whose career has spanned six decades. He first emerged as a vocalist in the mid 1960's with string of top hits. When he came on stage, he gyrated his body and the girls would scream*

uncontrollably. *Later he toured regularly, made appearances in Las Vegas (1967-2011), and in 2012 had a career comeback coaching on UK version of The Voice UK. His voice has been described as a full-throated, robust baritone. He was a tantalizing singer, somewhat like the Elvis of Wales.*

Well, every Wednesday night at 8 pm the Tom Jones Show came on. Only a few of the nursing students had televisions, so most of us crowded into Pam's room. We had to wait for the matron to be on her break and then be incredibly careful not to make too much of a ruckus. There were no PVR's to record in those days as there are now in the 21st century.

I did well at nursing for the first while and I enjoyed the clinicals, but when I went back to my room there was no one there and it was so quiet. Who can study in the quietness? I was not used to that because of growing up with a noisy sibling. Well, I had a good time for a few months but I didn't apply myself to the work and was asked to leave at the end of three months. There were so many rules and restrictions and it was just like living at home, but not at home. I did have a fabulous time while I lived in residence. It was great being away from home, but I forgot one part of the equation you must study So, the proof was in the puddling. I was devasted when I was asked to leave mostly because I was embarrassed to face the music with my parents and other relatives with the news that I had failed.

"The proof of the pudding is in the eating" is an old proverb. The Oxford Dictionary of Quotations dates it to the early 14th century, albeit without offering any supporting evidence for that assertion. The phrase is widely attributed to Cervantes in his book **The History of Don Quixote**.

I remember now that failing is a good thing; it means you attempted something. You always must try and if it does not work, try something else. No great individual has succeeded without failing. One thing I have learned from "failing" is I know that if I had never tried a nursing career, I would not have known that I could carry on and try again. Failing allowed me to try something else and find my own path. I did have the option at that time to re-apply and enter the next class in September 1970, a two-year program, so I would have graduated at the same time as my other classmates, but I was too proud and embarrassed at the time so I left and chose another path. I am sure life would have been a great deal different if I had decided to go into the new two-year program, but "pride goeth before the fall".

*This comes from **the Book of Proverbs**. In the King James Version of the Bible, it reads, "Pride goeth before destruction, and a haughty spirit before a fall. Some theologians interpret this to mean that a proud person will be condemned to hell. Things in life always happen just as they are supposed to happen. Pride certainly goes before the fall.*

1969

Well, my Dad picked me up from the nurses' residence and loaded my great big blue metal trunk into his car and off we went home again. He was very accepting of me coming home. He did not scold me; he was great. I was embarrassed but also glad to be out of there. When I look back, I know that it had a lot to do with my not focusing on what I was there for. I was having too much of a good time being away from home even though it was only across town. This was another regret. I should have gone to a school of nursing out of province.

I guess sometimes regrets can be life lessons learned or experiences. Choices are quite often hind sight. There I go again with the would have, should have, or could have. We are all so prone to in our lives.

How should "would' and "could" and "should" be used? English grammar texts say that they are all auxiliary verbs that need to be paired with a verb (action word). They are used as the past tense of "shall", "will" and "can" but are also used in other situations.

Just let the cards fall, and pick up the pieces and move on. That must be the gypsy in me coming out again. I do believe this is what has allowed me not to be overly reactionary when tragedy has entered my life and my career. I worked in an area of life that was somewhat dangerous. I was never alone but there was the risk of being attacked or injured permanently by the clients I was attending. Some of my colleagues commented "You just never get frazzled in these tough situations". I never did. I am thankful too that I didn't get hit or injured, not saying other coworkers provoked clients (some of them did), but I was very careful not to do that and would tell them straight up what was the plan and focus for the treatment being offered to them.

The first morning after I left nursing school, I went to my best friend Marla's place. All these years later, we still are closest and best friends. I spoke with Marla's sister, Olga, who told me to go to Bathurst Containers for a job interview since they needed someone there to do the typesetting and reception. The only office experience I had was at Nielsen Clearing House, which did not seem like office work to me. I did not type well, did not do shorthand, but I thought that I probably could file. I was convinced by the two sisters to go and try for it. After all, I had just been asked to leave the nursing school and I could not stay at home. All I can say now, looking back, they must have been desperate. I was successful and got the job and quite enjoyed it.

Shortly after I got the job, my father was transferred to Edmonton, Alberta, with his work so I decided to stay behind and continue working. This was my opportunity to be independent and make all my own decisions. Sometimes they were not always the wisest ones. I had the use of my mother's blue 1969 Acadian, so I could drive to work every day. This car saw a few more miles on the odometer than it would have had if my mother had stayed behind. There were a few return trips to Fredericton on the same night. I got around though: Fredericton a few times, down to Grand Bay and to Dipper Harbour where Marla's family had a house by the ocean.

I could go to Dipper Harbour where Marla's family had a house by the ocean. Once my friends knew I had a car, they often asked to be driven around, but I did not buy in to it every time. After a bit, I realized that I had become a bit of a taxi driver so thought maybe it would be best to send the car out west. Our house was eventually sold and I had to find other accommodations. Reg and Dolly White were my new surrogate family since this is where I landed for awhile. This was a time for me to sow some wild oats. I never really knew what that meant. I was always a little naïve and I think that served me well all my life.

1970

I lived in the family house for awhile until the movers came to pack up all the family possessions. Then I had to find a place to live. While living in Saint John after my parents left, I boarded with Dolly and Reginald White who were the parents of Randy White the future Reform Party Member of Parliament for three years. Randy later joined the new Conservative Party, so looking back, I can say that I was staying with celebrities. Dolly was into reading tarot cards and liked to raise card tables to ask questions of people who had departed this earth. My Dad loved this couple and was very intrigued by Dolly and her table raising. He even thought he could do it too. Reginald worked for my father in the glass shop, so there was a bit of a connection. They were happy to have me living with them. It was a fun fit.

I shared a room with a friend who was a mate from our church. She was a rebel in her own right. And she had a boyfriend who much older than we were but it was a bit of a status to have an older boyfriend. I went on a few road trips with them, once to St. Stephen's and that was one that I regret. Luckily, it turned out alright for me. They had fixed me up with a friend of my friend's boyfriend who I now realize was a much older man who was looking for some fun in the hay. We ended up in a motel, but I was not going to have any of this, so he was kind and respected my innocence. We just hung out until the other two were ready to leave and head back to Saint John. I was never so glad to get back home. I sure got myself into some awkward situations. Another time, we went to Fredericton with them and they got a hotel room and so did we, and once again I dodged a bullet. I made sure I did not get into that predicament again. How does it go" Once bitten twice shy.?"

Reggie, Dolly's husband, used to tease me about not having a boyfriend. He would say, "You will know. One day the bells would go off in your head. You will know he's the one."

It probably is another one of my regrets, but I will have to live with it. My roommate had a boyfriend and all of her other friends did too. Since I had no romantic entanglements, I thought I would leave town and see what was out on the west coast, at least as far as Alberta. Maybe I would find Mr. Right or Mr. Wrong. I did realize that I was giving up my new-found freedom, but I was willing to do it to see the west. Keep in mind my imagination of the west was from a picture in a grade six geography text book with a derrick oil pump in the picture.

I was working in the mighty city of Saint John and I was all alone and except for my roommate and my friend Marla. I had no family on the East Coast and I had no love interest as such. I liked my job at Bathurst Containers as the typesetter for the boxes but I was sure there was something wonderful waiting for me in the west. So, I was heading out of town for the mighty prairies of Alberta. I was quitting my job and going to points unknown. Something I later regretted when I would arrive in the city of Edmonton but I would get over it.

CHAPTER TWELVE

Westward Ho!

When my parents left for Alberta, they decided to send my mother's car by rail. I tell you this because the cost of sending the car by train to Edmonton came with a first-class ticket to for me, or someone else, to travel also. It included meals and a roomette for me.

I did not have to sleep in an upper bunk. I could travel first class. I even ate in the fancy dining room with fine linen, silver service, and waiters in their white jackets. Travelling first class was an attraction. I stayed in Saint John until July and then made plans to head west by train to find out what was so special about Alberta. I had had a picture in my head about what it would look like based on a Grade Six geography book. I thought Alberta was just open prairie and oil derricks.

I got on the train with all my belongings loaded in my big blue metal trunk and headed west. My dear friend Marla and her parents came to the train station to see me off. I did not know when I would see them again. It was another step into my Gypsy lifestyle. I guess I did have a wild side, or better still, an adventurous side. I was cautious but still wanted to try things out.

While on the train, I became acquainted with one of the porters. Robert was his name,I think only think because it was over 50 years ago and he was from Winnipeg. I knew him for only about three days, the length of the trip from Montreal to Winnipeg before he got off and headed back east. He was a university student working the trains for summer employment to pay his university tuition. He was an English major. He gave me a book, the Man from La Mancha which I read and have read a few times since. The story line is a little like my own life. I am not sure who my manservant is to be though, my knight in armour awaits me.

Man of La Mancha *During the volatile days of the Spanish Inquisition, the writer, Miguel de Cervantes (played by Peter O'Toole in the movie version) and his manservant (played by James Coco) make their living as tax collectors, but soon find themselves imprisoned after being accused of crimes against the church. Now facing the wrath of their fellow inmates, Cervantes must persuade the unruly bunch not to burn his prized manuscript – so he performs it for them. With the help of a prostitute (played by Sophia Loren), they begin the tale of Don Quixote and Sancho Panza. Years later, when I finally saw the movie version on the big screen, and it made the book come alive.*

I guess this was where my fascination with trains began. Even to this day I enjoy riding the trains. When my girls were little, I thought I would get them a train set to put under the tree at Christmas time but they were not as interested as I was.

I had a friend for awhile who was really into trains. He was part of a train group that met every week and would take turns meeting at each other's home and do train runs on each other's set ups. He had a train village that went around the entire basement of his home. It was amazing.

I have had many train rides all over the world over the years. I think one of the best and most interesting trips anyone could experience was when my husband and I went to India. My daughter, Jessica, met us in New Delhi at the airport with our grandson in her arms. We spent a night in the hotel and then headed out the next day for Varanasi on the train. An overnight 17 hour train ride.

2007 another train experience

We rode the train from New Delhi to Varanasi, an overnight ride of about 17 hours. We had several suitcases with us containing donations and supplies for Jessica's school my work colleagues had give us. One of the things Jessica had asked for was underwear for the little girls. We got donations from a few pharmacies of over-the-counter medications that we near expiration date but were still usable. We had in total about 8 suitcases which were filled with donations from my workmates at the mental health office where I worked. It was amazing the our pouring of generosity from my friends personal lives. One pharmacy donated some almost outdated over the counter medications. The sight at the airport was like no other since today we would not be able to take as many suitcases on without a charge. There was no extra charge. I think there must have been some divine intervention.

Some interesting facts about New Delhi

- *Delhi and New Delhi are technically two different places. Delhi is a city and a union territory of India with a population of more than 16 million while New Delhi is a city within that area with 11+ million people (2016). Delhi is the second most populated city in the world. It is home to 18 billionaires and 23,00 millionaires. The city experiences frequent earthquakes*
- *Delhi is the home to the largest market of spices in Asia*
- *The Delhi Transport Corporation along with other public transport services in Delhi is entirely run on Compressed Natural Gas (CNG)*
- *Delhi is the leading commercial center of India*
- *Delhi is home to a unique Museum of Toilets*
- *Delhi hosted the most expensive Commonwealth Games to date in 2010*
- *New Delhi is home to the world's tallest brick structure.*
- *Winter generally begins in November and peaks in January. (source: Wikipedia)*

Now in our section of the train, there were three tiers of bunks. We did not have a compartment all to ourselves and were mixed in with people from every walk of life. One man, a university professor, was travelling with his wife. Also, there was a young family, a mom, Dad, and three young boys and the four of us and we all had to have a place to sleep. I made sure I did not sleep on the top bunk. There were chai sellers who came around all during the trip and others offered rice and dahl and biryani (traditional rice and veggie dish). It was like a moving smorgasbord travelling across India.

When it was time to go to sleep, porters came around with clean, white, ironed sheets for every bunk bed which were in brown paper packages. That was probably the most sanitary part of India. Another interesting part of the sleeping arrangements was that if you were assigned to the middle bunk you had to go to bed when the bottom bunk people headed to bed since there would be no place to sit. Everyone was very accommodating though. No one made a fuss and it all went off like clock work. The trip to the bathroom was an interesting journey. The ride across the country was rough, but the bathroom was typical of Indian standards with a stainless-steel toilet which was a hole in the floor of the moving train. You had to hang on for dear life when you squatted over the hole to pee or do number 2 or else you would go flying across the tiny bathroom and out the door if you had not locked it when you had entered.

July 1970

When I arrived in Montreal on my cross-country trip, I had to change trains, and I had pre-planned to stay there for a week with my parents' friends Harold and Charlotte Schultz and visit the fine city of Montreal. I had the time of my life; I will always hold this time with Harold and Charlotte dear in my heart. I was treated like a princess and taken to all the finest restaurants and all the sights of the city. When it came time to leave it was a sad moment. I wanted to stay and get a job, but I was on my way to Edmonton and the family was waiting for me there.

Montreal is such a gem of a destination. Located on the St. Lawrence River, it has prospered as a cosmopolitan hub of communication and trade. Jacques Cartier landed there in 1535 and took the territory for King Francois I of France, but it was not until 1642 that Paul de Chomedey founded a small mission station called Ville Marie de Mont-Réal

These are some of the places I visited on my excursions in Montreal.

- Basilica Notre Dame which is the most significant landmark of Montreal. The Gothic Revival undertaking was designed by an Irish Architect James O'Donnell and built between 1824-29. The thriving Catholic church has a stunning medieval style interior that features walnut carvings, exquisite stained-glass windows, and 24 carat stars in a vaulted blue ceiling, as well as one of the largest Casavant organs in North America.
- Musée de Beaux Arts de Montreal is one of the most impressive museums in North America. It began life in 1860 when a group of collectors set up the Art Association of Montreal to present exhibitions, and establish an art school.

I have not been back to see Montreal since this visit aside from driving through on a cross Canada road trip.

Years later Harold told my Dad he so wanted me to stay. This lovely couple did not have any children of their own, and we had really connected. Hindsight always tends to present itself at the most inopportune time. I think I should have stayed there, found a job, and learned to speak French. That would have been a major asset in my career path. I have always been someone who holds back and puts off deciding. Another lesson to keep in mind. Follow your dreams not someone else's. Should have would have could have the best words said by many.

This also makes me think of when I had just gotten my driver's license and a friend of ours, Jean Foss, was at our house, I am not sure why she did not have her car, but I had been volunteered to drive her home after the visit. It has always stuck in my mind what Jean said next, "He who hesitates is lost!" I looked at her and thought, "Yes, go Susan! Go Susan!" and since then I have always thought of Jean when there has been an inkling of hesitation. One of my desires for a career was to become an airline stewardess but at that time you had to speak French, and you also had to be trained as a nurse with some companies.

Here are some of the stringent guidelines that Pan Am laid out.

*During **Pan Am's** heyday in the 1960s, there were strict requirements for stewardesses. They had to be at least 5-foot-2, weigh no more than 130 pounds, and retire by age 32. They could not be married or have children, either. As a result, most women averaged just 18 months on the job. In the 1970s, the organization Stewardesses for Women's Rights forced airlines to change their ways. The mandatory retirement age was the first thing to go. By the 1980s, the marriage restriction was gone as well. These days, if flight attendants can do the job and pass a yearly training program, we can keep flying. As for weight restrictions, most of those disappeared in the 1990s. Today, the rules are about safety: Flight attendants who cannot sit in the jump seat without an extended seat belt or cannot fit through the emergency exit window cannot fly. The same goes for height requirements: We must be tall enough to grab equipment from the overhead bins, but not so tall that we are hitting our heads on the ceiling. Today, that typically means between 5-foot-3 and 6-foot-1, depending on the aircraft. Most of these guidelines would be forbidden today with all the political correctness we are part of today. (Source: Wikipedia)*

The Schultz's took me to the most amazing tourist destinations in Montreal. There was another couple that went with us for the evening dining and even on the shopping sprees that Charlotte took me on. She thought I should buy a wig. They were all the rage then, so I did buy one. It was streaked, but I do have a pumpkin head so it was difficult to make the darn thing stay on. I also was encouraged to purchase these short dresses called skorts. They were shorts with a top to match, but looked like a shorter dress. I am quite tall so my height was accentuated with the short, short skirt. This was probably the first time I was so frivolous in shopping but I did have some high style ladies encouraging me. It was so much fun.

I was in a hurry to get to the west to see my parents and grandparents. I did not know why, but well one reason was I did love my family. They always made me feel obligated to be there. Guilty is more like it. That is how I perceived it. I think truly the love of my family was more like it.

Years later, I learned that guilt is something a person puts upon themselves. It has nothing to do with anyone else. It is one of the most common, but least understood of emotions. When the guilt becomes chronic, it can contribute to chronic mental health.... and I did allow guilt to rule a large part of my life. I finally saw the light. A little late but then again.... never too late. Remember Life is not a dress rehearsal there is not a replay button.

CHAPTER THIRTEEN

The Journey Westward Conintues

The journey across the prairies was yellow and more yellow. It was quite beautiful, and the wind was blowing through the stalks like dancing spirits. It was early morning when we crossed the Saskatchewan prairies and I sat on my bed in my roomette with the blind up to watch the sunrise over the landscape behind us. with the blind up to see the grain flowing in the wind. The heads of grain looked like they were ready to explode. So many people think it is boring crossing the prairies, but it was mesmerizing, the vastness and the openness. You could see forever and not be sure how far or long that really was. The charm of the "forever" has remained as strong and clear as it was the first time. I felt that "It will be here a forever" moment. This is my rambling as I tend to do sometimes.

I love it when you can see for ever. I am not like the rest of my family who love the mountains; they are beautiful but there is a certain amount of restriction. I always feel a little claustrophobic with mountains all around me.

When I arrived in Edmonton I was greeted by my parents and grandparents. They were all bright-eyed and so glad to see me. All four were asking me questions at the same time. How was your trip? Who did you see on the trip? Did you have great time in Montreal with Harold and Charlotte.?

I did not get a job for a week or so. I spent some time getting used to my new surroundings, unpacking, and getting sorted. I wanted to work; I wanted a job.

My parents had bought a huge house so we all could live together, meaning the four of us along with my grandparents who also had uprooted from their home in Halifax to move out west with my family.

Edmonton certainly did not look like the picture that was in my Grade six geography book which showed a picture of very flat country dotted with oil wells and the derricks pumping the oil. Edmonton is a very lovely city but very flat. You can see it from a distance many miles away across the very flat land. Did I mention it was flat? It isn't quite as flat as Saskatchewan, but Alberta is flat too.

My Dad was still selling glass for a company called Pilkington Glass, a company that was across Canada and the world too. One of his contacts was Rusco Windows and Doors in the north end of the city of Edmonton, so he suggested I apply for a job as receptionist there, and of course I was successful. A feather in my hat. I always seemed to get the job. I had horseshoes coming out of everywhere when it came to getting a job. I had applied for a couple of other jobs but this one came through so it was the one to set my destiny.

My job would be greeting visitors and answering phones. The former receptionist had quit and there was a long gap before I was hired, so when I started, I discovered that no one had done any filing for an awfully long time. There was an enormous pile of unfiled papers almost up to the ceiling in the office. No, I cannot stand clutter to this day. I even like to keep my garage tidy in case some one drives by when the door is open. That could be classified as OCD (obsessive compulsive disorder), just a little, maybe.

*What is OCD? **Obsessive-compulsive disorder (OCD)** is a disorder in which people have recurring, unwanted thoughts, ideas, or* sensations (obsessions) that make them feel driven to do something repetitively (compulsions). The repetitive behaviors, such as hand washing, checking on things or cleaning, can significantly interfere with a person's daily activities and social interactions.

Many people without OCD have distressing thoughts or repetitive behaviors. However, these thoughts and behaviors do not typically disrupt daily life. For people with OCD, thoughts are persistent, and behaviors are rigid. Not performing the behaviors commonly causes great distress. Many people with OCD know or suspect their obsessions are not realistic; others may think they could be true (known as limited insight). Even if they know their obsessions are not realistic, people with OCD have difficulty disengaging from the obsessive thoughts or stopping the compulsive actions.

I was also responsible for greeting visitors and answering the phones. The office manager was a bit of an old maid who, to put it bluntly, nagged. Oh, another thing she was a nosey parker. Well, her name was Gladys, not glad ass.??

While working there I was introduced to all the salesmen. I had to know their names and the specific details of what they did, since when I received phone calls, I needed to know which one to give the call to. One of them was named Frank. Does not sound all that exciting, but there he was, all his 6'4" of him. I was attracted to him because I had finally found someone who was taller than me, and he did seem nice and polite. He was very shy, and tall. I know I repeated the tall but it was very important. That was the first thing that attracted me to him. How shallow is that eh! I was 5'10" so a short partner was not in order. Height shouldn't be a factor, but I had only really dated a few men in my short life and I wanted someone I could look up to.

I remember a story Dad told about my now-departed Auntie Grace who was proposed to by a young man who was shorter than her and she said she couldn't possibly date or even marry someone who was shorter than her. Aunt Grace did find a tall man a short time later, our handsome Uncle Ludwick.

I had had mostly girl friends and was waiting for Mr. Right. Isn't everyone? In high school, I went out with this guy who was just my height so that was kind of okay but "better to have someone to look up to." I say, again. That is what I told my daughters years later, when they asked me, "Why did you marry Daddy?" I always answered, "because he was tall". They probably do not remember that now. They also used to ask, "Do you think he is handsome?" My answer, "Oh yes my darlings, he is better looking than even Clint Eastwood." As the years have progressed he has really got to look like Clint, how does that work?

I took a shine to Frank right off the bat. He was the owner's son at the company where I worked, I found out later. He always said he was not a very good salesman and has continued to say that he could not sell, forever, in all circumstances in his life. It was mostly because he was shy and lacked self confidence. No matter how much I told him he could do it and praised him for his good job in all areas of his life, he would not take any praise. No matter how many times I said, "You are good at it" and many other encouraging statements, he never believed me, or anyone else, that he could succeed at anything. This feeling came from within, and there was a lot of baggage that had created these feelings. We shared a lot of that baggage from both sides of our lives over the years. His father was a lovely man but ridiculously hard on Frank. His Dad never managed to offer much praise for anything he had done.

Frank can play the guitar very well, but he never thought he was good at that either. Years later in the marriage, he wanted ways to earn extra cash and I suggested he could teach guitar lessons but of course he thought that he was" wasn't' good enough." Obviously these feelings need to also come from within.

 *I will not give up as **Winston Churchill** had said" "This is the lesson: never give in, never give in, never, never, never, never—in nothing, great or small, large, or petty—never give in except to convictions of honour and good sense.*

I met Frank in August 1970.

Frank and I have had a crazy life. It all started out ordinarily. We dated for some time. Well, not that long. We met in August and dated until May of the following year and then I began thinking that this was not going anywhere, so I asked him point blank, "Are you leading me down the garden path or is this going somewhere?" I do think he was a little shocked. So, he asked me to marry him. Or did I ask him?

Another neighbour, had said to me one day when I was thinking I would never find Mr. Right" "You will know, the bells will go off. in your head and you will know that he is the right person." I know I am repeating myself but this is where Mr. Right appears. Frank and I got a long right from the start. I had wanted to ask him out, but girls didn't do that in the early 1970's, but I did. I finally got enough nerve to invite him to an Oktoberfest celebration at the country club where my parents belonged. This was our first date. It should have been called a Sadie Hawkins dance.

***Sadie Hawkins Day** is the day when the girls are supposed to ask boys out. Many people my age have vivid memories of those dreadful Sadie Hawkins Day school dances, where the pressure was on and the gossip was flying about who would ask whom to the dance. The legend that we have always been fed is that Sadie Hawkins Day is supposed to make girls and women feel a sense of empowerment. But once you know the ugly truth behind its origin, you will wonder why this atrocious "holiday" is still being observed today. The idea for Sadie Hawkins Day came out of a cartoon strip called L'il Abner about life in the backwoods of Appalachia and was drawn by Al Capp. In the strip, there was one day in November when unmarried women in the town of Dogpatch could chase the bachelors and "marry up" with the ones they caught.*

If I do go to this Oktoberfest event, I needed a new dress so I "seconded" my grandfather who lived with us to make it. Grandpa Oscar, "Gran Gran" to us kids, was a tailor by trade and he agreed to make the dress for my first date with Frank. Grandpa Oscar was thrilled. He would do anything for me and he did everything in his power to fulfil this wish. He was another amazing person in my life. He was my mother's father and he totally doted on me. He thought I could turn water into wine, which sounds a little sacrilegious, but whatever I did he was totally in awe of and supported me and bragged about me to all the relatives. This did a whole lot for my self-esteem.

I loved my grandparents and cannot say enough about them and how good they were to me. Gran Gran played the piano by ear, something which I could not do. I could play though, and he would love to listen to me play from time to time when they came to our place. It was like having two sets of parents; I was so lucky. I did spend a lot of time with them. My grandmother was a great cook and their house was a "go to" for a refuge minding my brother..

As a very young girl, they had always been there and always supported me when I was having difficulty with anything. When things were in a turmoil at home, I would head over to my grandparents' house. They only lived about two blocks away. We used to live at the bottom of their street then we moved even closer across the boulevard next to the church we all attended, St. Phillips Anglican church.

My brother probably was a good kid inside, but he has never showed this side of himself. There actually was a short window of time when we did get along. I tried to include my brother's wife, in some of my outings with my girlfriends but it did not work. There was a time when we all got along not sure what went wrong. We went to see the Vagina Monologs with Jan Arden once. Maybe it was too risqué for her. I thought we all had a great time" My mother had a book full of expressions that she tabulated over the years and the one that goes here so well would be: "You can't go back! Life goes on!!".I don't really believe these are steadfast in life and reality. Sometime when things are left a long time it gets harder to renew. Let's hope we mend our fences.

I should have been wise to the fact that Frank was late for our first date, and he has been late ever since for any occasion. He was late for our wedding. This was not totally his fault as his brother who was the best man insisted that they stop on the way to the church to get a disposable camera.

Most of all though, Frank was late to pick me up for our first date because he had been given incorrect directions by the secretary at work, Gladys! I guess Frank could not find the address, so he had to call Gladys at home. Now the cat was out of the bag. Gladys had given him the wrong directions so it took him forever to find my place. My Dad kept saying, "When is Ralph coming to pick you up?" I had no idea who "Ralph" was. There was a young man named Ralph who worked at Dominion Stores when I worked there but I am sure that was not the connection as that was many years before. To this day, I have no idea where he got the name Ralph from, except when I was in high school, I was sweet on this fellow whose name was Ralph Yeoman. We never did hit it off romantically, but he was pretty good looking, and we were always friends.

I always wondered what happened to Ralph. My parents frowned on being mixed up with anyone who was Catholic, and this was Ralph. Later, it was James Lynch. He was so handsome, and I really thought he was my true love. He was tall, good looking, and very funny. He was always blushing too. We never officially dated, but we did hang out with all the other teenagers who worked at the Dominion stores after school and on weekends. I think it was when I heard my parents say, "You can't be associating with people who are Catholic" that I decided to end a potential relationship with James. I ended it badly and did not give him any reason. I just stopped hanging around him. The irony in this is that Frank was Catholic.

I just must include another flashback of a story already mentioned. All I can say is this was really imprinted in my brain's memory, and I couldn't believe I let it happen.

Ralph had a friend named Harvey and one night when the two drove me and my friend Aida Craig home, we were listening to music and dancing in my front room until I thought it best to send them home. Unbeknownst to me, either Ralph or Harvey had taken the extra house key from the top of the fridge. Because my parents were away, I slept across the road at a neighbour's. I discovered the next morning that after I had gone to bed they came back into the house and took all my mother's decorative bulrushes out of a vase, put them on the carpet, and walked all over them spreading them everywhere and making a huge mess. Oh, I was initially horrified. Fortunately, my parents and grand parents were not due back from their trip to Saskatchewan for a while. I quickly cleaned up and went to work the next day. The two boys, now grown men of course, were quite sheepish when they approached me to return the house key when I arrived at work the next afternoon.

The Oktoberfest proved to be a success, even though Frank was late picking me up. I had the tickets and knew where to go. We were both very shy on this night. I wanted to go somewhere and have some fun. I still really did not know anyone in Edmonton even though I had arrived in July and this was October. The only other person I knew was Gladys and she was nobody's friend. We sat by themselves as most people were with groups of friends. We had the entire evening on our own, so we had to talk to each other since we could not really talk all that much at the office. I do not remember if there was much conversation between the two of us, but there was a lot of smiling and lowkey conversation. We really did not know each other except for the fact I was the receptionist at work. That was okay. I had not had much alcohol in my life, but this night I tried drinking beer. After all, it was an Oktoberfest, so you drink beer.

The country club had large jugs of beer on all the tables and, of course, I thought I would make an impression by keeping up with Frank in the beer drinking department. I had not eaten anything most of the day because I was saving up for the wonderful buffet yet to come. I discovered later in the evening that this was a bad move to go to a beer fest and a buffet on an empty stomach. We danced all night and ate lots of food. This was probably the last time I remember Frank dancing until we were living in Fort Smith in the Northwest Territories years later.

At the end of the evening, we headed home and for some unknown reason, Frank needed to drop by his apartment to pick up something. Well, when Frank was doing whatever it was that he was doing, I became very tired and started to feel unwell. I decided to lie on Frank's roommate's bed. That was not a good move either. All of a sudden, I felt the room spin, my tummy whirled, there was this great rush and I threw up all over Tommy's bed. Oh, this seemed like a disaster at the time, but Frank and I scurried about the apartment and got the bed all cleaned up. How embarrassing it was. This was not the best first date impression I had hoped to leave imprinted in Frank's mind.

We headed out to take me home and more disaster. Frank got a flat tire on his turquoise '62 Chevy Biscayne. What a beast. I finally got home, crept into the house, and didn't wake anyone. Oh, I forgot to mention that my dress, the one that my grandfather made for me, was all autumn colors. It was beautiful, made from this soft flannel like material. He did such a wonderful job and I wore red pumps. I looked so cute. The only fault I had with it was it has a sash for a belt and I always felt I looked like a bag tied in the middle. To this day, I feel like this. What a first date, a night to remember.

On Monday morning when we both arrived at work, separately of course, Gladys gave us a strange look and of course she had told Ken Lee, the Edmonton office boss, (not Frank's Dad) about us going out on Saturday night.

We blushed and spoke briefly and that was all. It wasn't until a week or so later that we did go out again, but it was never anything splashy, Frank didn't prove to be very creative with his date suggestions. Not a romantic bone in his body. We usually just went to his apartment and hung out with Tom and Dal, his room mates. It became a pattern. They would make supper and I would be invited most evenings. I remember the first meal they prepared. It was a big bowl of spaghetti and a big bowl of boiled potatoes. No sauce. Just that mashed potatoes and plain spaghetti just as I said. Men and their dietary habits. They have improved considerably I must say. Now Frank makes a mean stir fry and a great grill cheese sandwich. So long as there is lots of sauces and spices.

CHAPTER FOURTEEN

First Job in the West

March 1971

The job at Rusco Industries came to an end when I got fired because I apparently had put the wrong size on an order for a window. I was called into Ken Lee's office and told my job had come to an end. I was just as happy to be leaving this job; things were getting serious with Frank and it would be better if I did not work in the same office.

I noticed a job ad for the TD Bank, so applied to work as the secretary in the North Edmonton Office. I didn't have any formal secretarial training but had been a receptionist at Rusco, and I had taken short hand in high school, something called ABC shorthand. Luckily, I always have agreed with Alexander Graham Bell's philosophy that, "When one door closes, another opens; but we often look so long and so regretfully upon the closed door that we do not see the one which has opened for us".

There is always something better waiting for you. Thanks Mr. Bell.

June 1971

Well, when the manager at the bank saw what kind of shorthand I practiced, he said I had to find other employment since he did not like the kind of shorthand I used. Lame excuse. He was not within his rights to do this but I did not say anything. I was embarrassed and once again did not speak up. Once again, I was happy to leave because I saw another newspaper ad for a Laboratory Assistant where I would be trained as a phlebotomist. It meant I would have to learn how to poke a needle into someone's arm and extract blood. This was a challenge, but I knew I could do it. I was always up for a challenge. In my new position, I was mentored by Veronica who was a laboratory technician. Later we became friends, and she was in my wedding party. This was indeed a great job. It was my eye opener to the world of medical careers. I enjoyed working with the public, talking to them, and making them feel better.

The first time I had to take blood, I had to pretend that it was not hurting me more than it was hurting the patient. There were some really sick patients. My first attempt was with a lady who had a tracheotomy; she weighed about sixty-nine pounds, and was on a respirator as well. I felt horrible poking her but I went for it. Her arm was quite scarred. I had to wear personal protective equipment because she was so high risk for other infections.

In addition, I also had to do the admissions blood work some days. My first day doing that work, I was a little shocked as well. A patient who stood 6'10" came into the room for admission blood work. She was tall and so slim, but on the hospital form the gender was checked as male. I did not say a word. She wore quite lovely fishnet stockings, a tight knit dress, and her makeup was done so well. She was there for a gender reassignment. This was a real eye opener into the world of humanity. I was pretty sheltered in some ways, but also insightful and compassionate.

The other benefit of this job was that I also got trained to do electro-cardiograms as well. The person who trained me for electro cardiograms was Sister Thibault. She was very tiny and precise woman who wore the white habit of a nun, complete with the headgear and all. She was incredibly wise and knowledgeable. Sister Thibaut was a member of the Sisters of Charity, and I had a lot of respect for her. This was the same order of nuns that taught me at l St. Vincent's High School for Girls in Saint John, New Brunswick.

While working at the Misericordia Hospital in Edmonton I made a lot of friends.

It was always paramount with me to make friends with Frank's roommates, and Tommy's girlfriend was an ER nurse in the same hospital so I had that connection as well. I made my way about the hospital in all the departments but the lab was especially interesting and I even thought of becoming a laboratory technician. I could have taken the course on-site, but no, I did not.

I was still dating Frank and as time went by, I wondered if he would ever ask me to marry him. Several friends got married and we attended the weddings, but Frank never asked me to marry him so I asked him to marry me, can you believe it. Gypsy Girl had broken all the rules of etiquette.

When it came to dating, a lot of the time I was the instigator. I had asked him out initially, and I used to call him to see if he wanted to go out. Although I now feel that this was him being extremely shy, I thought at the time that he might be just leading me down the garden path. Back in the day, to be 22 and still not married was just not heard of. That is why I decided to ask him to marry me. A lot of water had gone under the bridge during our courtship, and I was getting tired of waiting to find out where the relationship was heading. When I asked him, he said, yes, and so our story continues. I still cannot believe I asked him. I was 23 when we finally did marry. Not sure why I was in such a hurry. It is all history now.

Frank did want to go and ask my father for his approval. This too was a little bit of tradition. Dad knew all about us and it was just a formality, but I was following the "book" on being engaged and this was one of the necessary steps to take before the wedding.

We had to attend three counselling sessions with the minister who would marry us so he could explain about the procedure and what to expect from marriage. This was a requirement of the Anglican Church. My wonderful mother-in-law arranged for two bridal showers: one was for bath supplies, and the other was for kitchen equipment. It was wonderful. I was blessed with a wonderful mother-in-law, but our connection was to last for far too short of a time.

Before Frank and I were married, we had to go to the provincial laboratory and have the Wassermann tests done to prove that we did not have any syphilis. This is not a requirement now, in the 21st century. The other requirement in those days was to have the Banns of Marriage that announced our intended marriage read out in church for three weeks in a row before the wedding. It was a public announcement giving people a chance to voice their opposition to the union. We did not really have to do this. There was a choice of either reading the bans or buying a license. We chose to do both.

*The **Banns of Marriage**, commonly known simply as the "**banns**" or "bans" /'bænz/ comes from a Middle English word meaning "proclamation" It is rooted in Frankish and then into Old French. The banns **are** the public announcement in a Christian **parish church** or in the town council of an impending marriage between two specified persons. The actual words spoken were, "If any of you know cause or just impediment why these persons should not be joined together in Holy Matrimony, ye are to declare it. This is for the (first, second, third) time of asking."*

February 1972

We were married in an Anglican church in Edmonton, Alberta. It was cold that day, so cold that the tires on the car that took me to the church were square from the frost. Frank was late getting to the church and everyone was a little panicky. As it turned out, his brother, David, had wanted to purchase a disposable camera to take pictures. So, they had to drop by a drugstore on the way. He ended up not even using the darn camera. The best laid plans of mice and men…. Well, in this case David was a doctor.

The date for the wedding was right in the middle of a frozen Alberta winter. I had wanted it to be in warm weather, but Frank could not get any holidays in the summertime. Frank worked for his father at Rusco Industries and he was not going to budge. Frank's Dad, who was also his superior, said he could not take any time off in the summer so that made it a little difficult to plan. Frank always seemed to be afraid of his Dad or anyone in authority. He would never ask anyone to change anything and does not like adversity of any kind. I suspect there had been a lot of adversity in house when he was growing up. So once again the plans tilted in Frank's favor. I never took a stand and said, "Yes, fine." and did not ruffle the feathers.

Frank's mother was Roman Catholic, and she particularly wanted a Catholic priest in attendance, so we found this amazing priest who was seen as a bit of a rebel in the Catholic Church. He agreed to go along with the family's wishes and participate with an Anglican minister from St. John's Anglican Church in South Edmonton. There were two interviews one with the Anglican minister, Father Bethel, who asked the two of us what percentage should each of us contribute to the marriage. We both replied with fifty percent each. Well, Father Bethel corrected us by saying we both needed to put in one hundred percent. That was a surprise to both of us, but makes total sense now. The interview with the Catholic priest was a little more relaxed and he only asked one question, "Who would be raising the children?" Of course, we both responded that I would be in charge. He felt that the children should be brought up in the faith of the mother. He was liberal for a Catholic priest.

The sad thing about my mother-in-law's request for this special service was that she had a heart attack two days before the wedding. She was not able to attend.

I did not have many really close friends yet. That was a dilemma. Who would I ask to be my bridesmaids? I did have Veronica, a close friend at work and so I asked her. Then I asked my old friend Marla from New Brunswick. She agreed happily when I asked, but then she herself got married in mid-January, on my birthday, in fact. She did manage to come to my wedding anyways even though she had just been married a month earlier. She and her mother, Dorothy, came together. I was thrilled and honoured; I loved her mother. It was special that they both came all the way across the country in the winter for my wedding. It was like having more family. They are both incredibly special to me.

Marla was remarkably close to me. I had spent a lot of time at Marla's house during my high school years. Sometimes when I did not feel well and did not go to school, I would go to Marla's house and her mother would write an excuse for me for the teacher. I was afraid to ask my mother. Maybe it was not fear but just that I knew my mother would say "no" and send me to school. My mother said "no" to me a lot but not to my brother. In retrospect however, I'd say that her saying "no" to me turned out well. I did learn about boundaries and a lot about respecting them.

Veronica, my other bride's maid, and I have lost touch over the years despite the fact that I tried to reconnect a few years ago, but nothing transpired. No fault on anyone's part just life and a mass pandemic.

My Grandmother Ella bought my wedding dress for me. The three of us, my mom, my grandma, and I, went to The Bay's Bridal Shop in Edmonton and I tried on a few gowns. The one I picked was very slim fitting and velvet. It was beautiful and had a long train with lace on it. I did look lovely. The bridesmaids' dresses were to be made from purple and lavender floral chiffon, so I sent the material for Marla to make her own dress and Veronica did the same. When Marla arrived for the wedding, the day before the rehearsal, she sat with her dress in her lap as she finished the hem.

The rehearsal dinner, hosted by my in-laws, was held at the Calgary Trail Hotel. It was a lot of fun. My Dad and Frank's Dad had a few too many drinks but that was excusable since their children were about to get married. It did not happen too often. In fact, the only other time I remember distinctly was when Jessica was born. Another opportunity to celebrate.

Frank's family bought him a new suit. It was a lovely brown suit and he looked so handsome, but for the wedding ceremony, he wore a black tuxedo. His brother was his best man. He was away travelling close to the time of the wedding so we hoped he would arrive home in time. He had finished just med school and was taking a break.

We were married in St. John the Evangelist Anglican church in Edmonton, Alberta. It was a great change from Nepal or Bali where he was travelling. It was a beautiful church and had a unique architectural design. Some people said it looked like an upside-down teapot. It had wonderful stained-glass windows, and the carpet was royal blue. Frank and I checked it out just a few years ago, and it is as lovely a structure as ever. It was special to be in the place we had been married so many years ago.

We noticed a few little cosmetic changes like new carpeting and a railing by the organist area. We had to have someone escort us inside the church. There is much higher security on most churches now. This is how life has changed in 40 years. Now we need security to enter churches.

Our wedding day was bright and white, but so cold. Thank goodness for my white velvet dress with the long velvet and lace train that went all the way to the floor. I looked great, and I did not resemble any gypsy I knew. It was -26 degrees below zero on the day we for married. That was mighty cold. The tires on the car had frozen square on the bottom overnight and the ride to the church was bumpy. I had my nurse's cape on my shoulders to keep me comfy. With my long white velvet gown, I was well clad for the frigid temperatures. It was fine, but darn cold.

The church was all decorated white satin bows on the ends of the pews and roses and carnations on the altar. At home, everyone was getting ready. My mother and grandmother helped me get ready.

Marla and her mother were fussing about as well. It was great to have them with us. They were family. Then my Dad got all teary-eyed when he was helping me into the car. This is such a wonderful memory to have all three generations present on my special day.

I was patiently waiting in the alcove room with my Dad. My mom had already been ushered into her place in the front row. Frank's father was up front on the opposite side of church. Frank was late arriving, and we all were a little panicky. As it turned out his brother, David, had wanted to purchase a disposable camera to take pictures, so they had to drop by a drugstore on the way and Frank was late, and he has been late ever since.

We had not picked the traditional wedding march, but rather something called Saraband by William Harris, the same music as at Princess Margaret's wedding. As a result, Frank did not look back as I was marching up the aisle on my father's arm. He did not look until I arrived at the altar, so he missed it all, the splendor and the glory of the beautiful bride marching toward him, with her beautiful bouquet, her flowing white velvet gown, and her long curled blonde tresses. I got a different hairdo for the big day, hair all curled and looking quite radiant and beautiful. Frank did not turn around until I was almost at the front of the church and he did not recognize me. Well, I think it was the wedding march that threw him off as it wasn't the traditional Here Comes the Bride". My mother-in-law the entire day because of a heart attack. She had always wanted her boys to get married. She said once" I want one wedding, just one." Well, she did get one wedding, but she was not able to be there.

The reception at the Derrick Country Club near our house was lovely. We chuckle today about our choice of wine for the wedding. It was Baby Duck and there was a bottle on every table, meant for the toasts to the bride and groom. Nobody drinks Baby Duck today; it is still sold in the government stores but those with a discriminating palate would not choose Baby Duck. It is like alcoholic pop. My father-in-law had a fun time at the reception. He always liked to be the center of attention as does my father.

Following the reception, my Dad invited a group of guests back to our house for refreshments and socializing. Quite a few came, and I was so surprised. Then, it was our time to get ready to leave on the honeymoon. I changed into my going-away outfit, a lovely brown suit and, of course, I did have an overcoat on since it was 30 below zero by the time evening came.

Marla and Veronica were absent for awhile after we got back to our house, but I did not notice because there was so much excitement. I discovered later that they had been up to no good.

Before we got to actually head out, the doorbell rang. Who could it be? It was my cousin and her husband, Lilly, and Havelock Sedman. They were invited to the wedding but, as Jehovah Witnesses, they are not permitted to attend weddings in other churches. They arrived with a wicker basket full of cookies, cakes, and of course, the tracts designed to persuade us to become Jehovah Witnesses. They thought this would be good reading on our honeymoon. We were very gracious and thanked them. They refused to stay and headed out down the sidewalk. We did not take the tracts with us, but graciously accepted the gift and did take the goodies in the car.

Before we headed on to Banff, we took a slight detour. We stopped at the Glen Valley Hospital and gave Mrs. Morwood, my new mother-in-law, all the details of the wedding. Her exceptionally good friend Nell Carter had caught the bouquet and had taken it to her at the hospital. This was so sweet of Nell. Everyone in the Morwood family loved Nell. She was also there when we arrived to see Sylvia. It was a lovely visit. I loved my mother-in-law. We only had her for a very few years, ten to be exact.

We spent our first night as a married couple at the Thunderbird Motel in Red Deer, Alberta, on the way to Banff, our honeymoon destination. The road conditions were horrible, and a blizzard made the visibility was even worse. We had already reserved the room, knowing what the road conditions could be on the Edmonton to Calgary highway. I had bought the most beautiful white negligée for my wedding night. It was expensive and I probably never wore again. I did not wear it awfully long that night either.

We had a short honeymoon in Banff, Alberta and stayed at he Banff Springs Hotel.

It was lovely and first class. We ate in the beautiful old-world dining room which reminded me of jolly ole England, a place I had only read about in books. The hotel 's rooms were not all that fancy but they were suitable for a honeymoon. I still think it was a fantastic choice for a honeymoon. We have never been back since except to enjoy the hot tub attached to the hotel.

When Frank and I arrived at the hotel in Banff, I found out where Marla and Veronica had been the night of the reception before we left. I opened my suitcase and found that those two lovelies had filled my clothes with corn flakes. Thank heavens there was no milk on the cornflakes, but they had taken the time and effort to sew them into my clothes. I laughed out loud when I saw this.

The next morning, we awoke to snow, so much snow that we could not see our car in the parking lot. Well, for newlyweds that was not a problem. That just meant we had to walk everywhere or just stay inside. We did not stay inside much though. We got up and went to Lake Louise one day and Sunshine Ski Resort another day for some great skiing. In the evenings, we went to the hot tub and then for dinner, either in the hotel or in the town. Some evenings we walked from the hotel into town.

We did not stay long. I only had 5 days holidays for our honeymoon because I had started a new job only about six months before the wedding. That was fine. We made sure we had made up for it through all the years that have followed.

Our wedding pretty much went without a hitch, except for the fact that my dear sweet mother-in-law was absent. There was one small flaw and that was only that Frank was late arriving with his brother. David and Frank are notorious for being late ... always. If that was and is the worst nothing to lose sleep over.

CHAPTER FIFTEEN

Working at the Misericordia

1972

I really enjoyed my new job at Misericordia Hospital in Edmonton where I did lab tests and electrocardiograms for about two years or so. It was day and evening shifts, so it was not always the most conducive situation for newly married life. The one thing that sticks in my mind about working there was when Liz, one of the student laboratory technicians, said, "Well, I will never be a nobody like the laboratory assistants". I am not sure if she knew that her opinion was heard or if she cared. I may have always felt like a nobody and just needed more education to prove myself years later, but that statement rang in my head for awhile.

We lived in a one-bedroom, basement apartment for the first six or eight months of our marriage. During this time, my father-in-law and one of his salesmen, John MacDonald, came for supper. The reason I tell you this is that Frank used to say I did not make my chili spicy enough, so I made a batch with lots of hot spices and put it in the freezer just in case there was someone coming to dinner. Well Mr. Morwood. surprised us, so we served our spicy chilli. Mr. Morwood. was very gracious and said he loved the chili but he did have tears running down his cheeks. I asked him if he would like a second helping and he declined, but John Mc Donald said that he would have more. He was such a brave soul. He literally had tears running down his cheeks too. Next batch, I did not put quite as much chili pepper.

It was not long before I got the bug to buy a house, so we went to an open house near the hospital where I worked. It was a perfect fit for us. The show home had red shag carpeting which was all the rage back in the 70's and there was a feature wall that was painted black. OH, it was so perfect! We had to have this place. We signed a contract on the condition of getting financing. We didn't even have a down payment. Hard to believe the price of the house. It was only $25,900 dollars. That isn't even enough for a down payment today in the 21st century. The next day after work, Frank dropped me at the bank so we could arrange a deposit. I was in and out in 10 minutes and we had the down payment we needed for the house. He was shocked to say the least. "How did you manage that?" said Frank. I guess I was good at convincing to the bank manager. Frank's name should have been Thomas, like Doubting Thomas.

Doubting Thomas. *One who is habitually doubtful. A* doubting Thomas *is a skeptic who refuses to believe without direct personal experience and refers to the Apostle Thomas who doubted Jesus's resurrection in the presence of ten other apostles until he had first hand personal evidence of it. (John 20:24-29)*

I still have no idea why Frank had this doubting attitude. I simply walked in and met with the manager. He gave me the loan, so we could arrange our financing for the new house. We had a small mortgage payment by today's standards. If I recall, it was $233.00 per month. We were both working, so it was no problem. To put the cost of living of things in perspective, I recall having a Grey Cup party in our little apartment and filling our grocery cart for about $39. That would barely fill one grocery bag today.

When we moved into our new house, the red shag carpet was great until springtime when all the mud was tracked in from the unpaved road outside. We did not yet have a lawn either. We did not paint the feature wall black though. We did have was an old black vinyl leather-like hide-a-bed that it matched the red shag fabulously. I did have a dishwasher from our one-bedroom apartment. It was our first big purchase. It was avocado green. In fact, I still believe that a dishwasher was a great purchase when two people in the household worked. My co-worker did say it would prevent colds and flu, so of course we had to have a dishwasher.

We had only been married just over a year, so we still did not have our new furniture. We did manage to have a housewarming. It was spectacular! We invited all the friends we could think of. The house was bursting at the seams. It was a great time. My parents came as well. I always invited them and sometimes they declined. They had a highly active social life. I always thought Frank and I did, but they were overboard. Our lives are pale by comparison.

The house was great, and it was pretty close to our work, that was one main reason why we chose the house in this location. It would have been ideal but I didn't like working the evening shift, so I changed jobs to work in the laboratory at the University of Alberta. Frank had straight days at first, but eventually he did take over his Dad's other glass company, Dual Pane. Then, he put the shop on shift work so they could produce more sealed units. It was a busy time for him as there was great competition going on in the city in the glass industry. The big companies eventually shut all the little producers out of the market, so Frank shut down Dual Pane Glass, and we were asked to move to Calgary to work with his Dad. I was a little disappointed since we had just bought a new house and I had started a new job.

1973

The new job at the university was another great job for me even though I was not working with people directly. It was with petri dishes and injecting mice with drugs for testing. I had to mix and make the agar for the petri dishes. This is where I felt at home and the people, I worked with were a fabulous group of individuals. I have always been fortunate to work with wonderful people everywhere I have been, and this was no exception. I wanted to stay there forever but.... my father-in-law had other ideas.

I worked at the university lab for some time until Frank was asked by his father to come and work for him in his Calgary office. This meant a lot of upheaval in our lives. We had just purchased our lovely brand-new home three months before and now would have to sell it. We had hardly had time to decorate, except for the already-installed red shag.

My Gypsy Life had started exceedingly early in my marriage. We decided to sell the house ourselves That meant doing it without a realtor. We put a sign in the window and about ten minutes later a man drove by and came knocking on the door. He asked to buy the house. We had never sold a house this way but neither had we owned a house before. He gave us full price. We did not know it was possible to sell a house in 20 minutes. Maybe real estate was our path......not. The move wasn't a mutual choice, but my husband said we were moving, so we moved. It did not prove to be such a good thing for us financially. We had only owned our house in Edmonton for about three months, so there was extraordinarily little profit when we sold, but we did have a down payment for our next purchase. It had always been my dream to live in the same house all my married life. Now, we did not have a place to live, so we decided it was necessary to bunk in with Frank's parents in Calgary until we found our next dream home.

We lived with Frank's parents for only a short time. We were hoping to find something close in town, near but not next door to his parents, but the prices were a little steep for us newbies. Frank's parents went on a trip to England and Scotland while we were living there and so we continued to look. We looked and looked all over Calgary before we found another place. It was in the east side of

Calgary, near Chestermere Lake. Although we wanted to be closer to the city, the prices were right for our down payment and our income. The house we chose was a brand-new split-level. We were happy with it.

We now had two cats: one a Siamese named Bing, and one a calico, named Grub. Grub got her name because she had been left out in the cold and her left ear was frozen off. It just seemed appropriate. You think that is a weird name, but it did suit her perfectly. The reason I mention the cats is because they had got out of the house at the same time, and both got pregnant.

Then one weekend, we left them alone on a weekend with enough food and water and when to last until we returned. When we got home, we could not locate them at first. We had a linen closet in our bathroom, so we thought maybe they were in there. Lo and behold, they had had their kittens in there and dragged them up to the top shelf so no one could get them. That was quite a feat. Later, we discovered that they had actually delivered the kittens on the lower level of the house, carried them all the way up two flights of stairs, and then somehow dragged them up to the top shelf of the linen closet. I think they were taking turns feeding them and not sure they knew which kittens belonged to which.

It was not too long after we arrived that I got job in a medical office working for a paediatric cardiologist. This was a serious job doing cardiograms on infants and young children. It was challenging. These patients had critical errors in their heart functioning. The doctor was genuinely nice, but a little stressed most of the time. He did not give any leeway for errors. The staff were fabulous too. I made some great connections. The location of the Calgary Associate Clinic on 6 Avenue SW was terrific. They had some interesting and archaic policies. If any female staff were pregnant, it was a written rule that they had to resign six months into their pregnancy. It may have been a safety issue too at that time. Remember this was the early seventies. Today women work up until the day of or the day before they are due. This may be, a little over the top but forcing people to quit because they are pregnant is a breach of human rights.

Hindsight again, I should have kept my big mouth shut and not told them my due date. Excitement overruled my better judgement. I did not look that pregnant until the very end of my term. I am relatively tall but have to say I have shrunk a little in height over the years. Being tall, the fetus was able to stretch out and I did not look all that pregnant. Being honest is always a good thing.

I was not in favor of this policy but I shared my due date and had to quit at my six-month mark. It was fine, but I did not know what I would do all day long while at home. Well, I found out. I did manage. I got things ready for the baby.

My friends from Edmonton wanted to put on a baby shower for me. That meant that I would have to drive up from Calgary in the old standard shift, orange Maverick car. I met the group at a restaurant and they showered me with gifts for the baby. Then, I had to drive home again, two hours on my own. My dear Dad was overly concerned that I was driving all that way on my own since I was eight months pregnant. It was all good.

I remember going on a picnic one Saturday with friends, Dal, and Lori, who already had one child. We went to a ranch on the outskirts of Calgary, and the men went horseback riding. I wanted to go too, but Ralph Hoar, the owner of the ranch, said no way, so I did not go. Ralph was just being extra cautious. On the way home, I had to ask Dal, a doctor, but an orthopedic surgeon, "How will I get this baby out of me?" It seemed like a strange question to ask but it was very puzzling at the time. Dal said, "Nature just takes its course, and the baby will find its way into the world." That was so true. I was very naive during my first pregnancy.

Shortly before the baby was born, Frank resigned from Rusco Industries and would not work for his Dad any longer. He felt he was at a crossroads in his life and decided to return to school to further his education. Frank decided to go back to Edmonton to take a Business Administration course at Northern Alberta Technical

Institute. He already had 4 years university, but that was not enough to get a well-paid job. Although he had first thought about taking up a trade such as plumbing, he opted for a Business Degree instead. Plumbing might have been more profitable.

CHAPTER SIXTEEN

Moving Back to Edmonton

We got a lot of flack from Frank's parents for jumping ship and moving back to Edmonton, but we had to look after ourselves. My parents still lived in Edmonton, so we would have them for back up, but we had to sell our house in East Calgary before we could make the move and settle in.

Once again, we were lucky enough to have a quick sale and so, we moved into a rental house owned by Grandpa Dave. This was in August and Frank started school in Edmonton on September 4th. Hmm what to do. We no longer had a house to sell so that was one less worry.

I was due Sept. 10th and Frank started school Sept. 4th. Bless her, my wonderful grandmother came out from White Rock, BC and stayed with me until I was due. I did not deliver until Sept 20th and had to be induced since Jessica was in no hurry to present herself to the world. So, my father-in-law, Dave and my wonderful mother-in-law, Sylvia, took me to the hospital. It was interesting to have the grandparents take me to the hospital, but it was quite lovely. It was a long night waiting for Jessica's to make her entrance. Before morning though, my little red-headed cherub had arrived.

When she finally appeared, we contacted Frank in Edmonton. He and my parents drove down immediately. Everyone was there in the hospital room already and I was not alone. When we were asked if we wanted to have the baby in the room with us over night, I was one of the weird ones who chose not to. I thought I would need this time to rest, and the nurses could do the job of bringing the baby to me for feeding.

Great excitement! That night, my father and Frank's father toasted Jessica Leigh and celebrated with the three women around. They said that Jessica was a trollop's name in the Bible so we would have to call her Jessica-Leigh, hyphenated.

But that is not true. **Jessica** *is a name of Hebrew origin meaning "gift", "God beholds". The name was first used in this form by Shakespeare in his play 'The Merchant of Venice' (1596), where it belonged to the daughter of Shylock. Shakespeare probably based it on the biblical name ISCAH which would have been spelled Jesca in his time.*

The two grandfathers were very inebriated according to my grandmother who very rarely touched spirits. But I do remember we took her to the Wheelhouse Pub years later for her 80th birthday. That was quite an eye opener for her. It was an exciting night for all…while I was in bed in the hospital recovering from all the trauma, they were frolicking in our house on Elbow Drive.

And so, we began our lives as a student couple, starving on a student loan. We had more free cash during those two years that Frank attended Northern Alberta Institute of Technology than we did sometimes when we were both working. We were so engrossed, or maybe that should be "engaged", Well, anyway we were busy looking after Jessica, our first little one, and Frank was terribly busy studying most of the time.

After Jess was born, I thought I would make a little money delivering mail for the Christmas rush. I managed to find help for babysitting with the lady next door on Saskatchewan Drive. I survived about 5 days and then I felt so much guilt for leaving my little baby with a stranger that I quit the job and stayed home. We managed on the student loan.

My mom and I did a few odd jobs. One was delivering phone books door to door on the south side of Edmonton. My mom was always up for a challenge. Jessica was wrapped in her snowsuit in the car seat, and I would drive to the addresses while mom would run up to the door. We took turns. My mom was a PISTOL. This did not pay much but it got us out of the house. It was fun doing crazy things with my mom. Sure do miss that little lady.

Mom and I did some interesting things. When Frank was in school taking his business administration program at NAIT, we were trying to pass the time by delivering phone books. We got paid but it was very little, and it was very cold. Jessica was with us, but we would take turns getting out of the car to run up the homes with a new phone book.

We were a struggling student couple with a newborn, and I did do a few jobs. I worked at Woodward's which is not longer in existence in the sporting goods department. My dear ole dad babysat Jessica who was barely walking while I worked, since my mom also worked at Woodward's too. Jessica was going to a babysitter for a few times until my dad was asked to pick her up this one day, when he arrived the husband had just given Jessica a swat on the behind and of course Grandpa witnessed this happening. He said "I will take her and not be bringing her back. No one hits my granddaughter." He is very protective of his children and grandchildren to this day.

Woodwards' *was a department store chain that operated in Alberta and British Columbia, Canada, for one hundred years, before its sale to the Hudson Bay Company (HBC). Woodward's was a central feature of the retail scene especially in southwestern British Columbia for much of the Twentieth Century. The chain was distinctive in that the stores included a large supermarket (the "Food Floor") as an adjunct at some of the department stores. When Woodward's sold out to Safeway, the flagship Food Floor began a reduced-size IGA store.*

When Woodward's sold the Food Floor - long known for its quality and its line of unusual specialities – to Safeway, the flagship food floor became a reduced-size IGA store until the building closed as Safeway showed no interest in that location. Many western Canadians fondly remember Woodward's famous "$1.49 Day" sales, held the first Tuesday of every month.

I think I got my Gypsy Fever naturally. My parents decided that they wanted to move into the house we were living in on Saskatchewan Drive in Edmonton. That meant that we had to find ourselves a new place to live. We were truly fortunate to find an apartment close to the house. It was ideal: two bedrooms, and two bathrooms, and a balcony. I could even walk to our former house and visit my parents during the day when Frank was in classes. It was a good move, although the packing and lifting and sorting were always a little challenging.

After graduation from Northern Institute of Technology, Frank was offered a job as Town Manager for Viking, Alberta, about 120 km from Edmonton, but he did not have to start for another month after completing his program. Luckily, we had saved some money and we decided to go on a trip of the Maritimes so I could show Frank my roots. We flew from Edmonton to Saint John and there we stayed with my girl friend Marla and her family. She is the friend who was my bridesmaid and came out to my wedding. She had two little boys already and I just had Jessica. We had a great time touring about.

We stayed for awhile with Marla, and then decided to go to Halifax where we visited other great friends, Norma, and Eric. We did not have a credit card at the time so we had to ask Eric to vouch for us so we could get a rental car. We stayed there for a short time and then travelled to Prince Edward Island where we visited with our friends the Birts. I was a friend of their daughter and we used visit in summertime and stay at the Proud's Cottages for a week. After work, my Dad would come home to the cottage after supper; the Birts also rented a cottage at the same time.

The highlight of the trip this time was the lobster feed. Oh, it was so good. I can still feel the melted butter dripping down my chin. This was a fabulous trip. We finished up the trip at St. Andrew's-by-the-Sea where I bought myself a wool poncho there which I still wear. We then drove back to Saint John and flew home. We had to get back to pack and move to Viking.

In 1976, when Frank became the Town Manager in Viking, Alberta, the population on the road sign read, 1225 people. Twenty years later, when we went back to Viking for a visit to see old friends, the sign read, 1055 people. That does not seem at all right. Didn't anyone know how to count in that town? We added one to the population during our time there, and I am sure others did too, but the population was decreasing.

Viking, Alberta, was the home of the famous hockey family, the Sutter's, one of the most famous families in the National Hockey League (NHL). Six brothers Brent, Brian, Darryl, Duane, Rich, and Ron reached the NHL in the 1970s and 80s. Four of the brothers, Brian, Duane, Darryl, and Brent, have gone on to become coaches and General Managers as well.

All the brothers played for either the Chicago Blackhawks or the St. Louis Blues at one point or another. A seventh brother named Gary is said by his brothers to have been the best hockey player of all seven boys, but rather than making his living as a hockey player, Gary stayed home to work on the family farm.

We had a great time living in Viking and the friends we made there are lifetime friends. While there I was pregnant with our second child and when I realized I was going to have to have baby in the tiny little hamlet I was shocked. The hospital was so small. I later lowered my standards and succumbed to delivering here. This is where our Karen was born. There was a funny incident in the middle of the night when the baby was brought to me for feeding. I was in a two-bed room and I was quite groggy at 3 am when the night nurse brought Karen to me. Luckily, I was awake enough and looked at the baby and thought this is not Karen. The baby belonged to the lady in the bed next to me. The funny thing was they looked very much alike, and both had a full head of red hair so it was a really innocent mistake.

It was not until Karen, our second daughter, was 12 months old that I went back to work. I went to work for a friend in his insurance office, one day a week. This gave me one day a week out of the house and a few extra dollars that I could call my own. We found a lovely grandmother-type lady, Mrs. Rattray, to come in and babysit the two little girls. When I say grandmother-type, she was a little old-fashioned and always wore a colorful apron, but she was very patient with the girls and listened to them. When I arrived home at about 5 pm every Thursday, Karen would be comfortably sitting on Mrs. Rattray's knee, listening to her tell a story.

The insurance office was on Main Street in Viking. The wall of my office backed onto the chiropractor's office, and he only came to town once a week, and of course it was on Thursdays. It was a busy little office on Thursdays. The farmers from the local area came in to make payments for their insurance and check on hail insurance and current rates, but the noise from the adjoining chiropractic office was like listening to a large popcorn popper at the movie theatre. Crack, pop, crack, pop. The chiropractor. was putting bones back in place.

I was always working at something, everywhere I lived. This was no different in the spring of 1978. The school buses in our area were short a few bus drivers. I had never done anything like this before. One of the local ladies approached me and asked if I would be interested in driving a school bus. "Oh," I said. I would have to think about that. So, I thought about it for a while. I would have to take a written test and a road test, but I decided to give it a try anyway. It was challenging to say the least, but I did it, passed the test, and became a school bus driver for a short while.

The first day of school was a nightmare. The bus was a 48-seater, a big one, and it had a standard transmission as well. I had had some practice, but the stick was a force to be reckoned with.

I was on time picking up the bus, but I must confess I was the last bus to arrive at the school. Our neighbour, Dennis, who just happened to be the school principal, was getting worried. There were a few other teachers in the school yard, waiting the arrival of my school bus. I was nervous all the way back. The passengers ranged in age from kindergarten to Grade 12, so there was a myriad of noises. The kids where chanting, yelling, and throwing sandwiches. Luckily, I never got hit with one, and there was a lot of heckling of the new bus driver. Dennis hopped on the bus when we arrived to see if I was alright. And yes, I was but a little rattled. But who wouldn't be with all that activity and this great big bus? I must admit it did get a little better as time went on. It was fun except the part when I drove in the winter months. I kept it up for about a year, and then Frank decided to change his job, so we moved to Surrey, BC. That was the end of Bus Driver Sue.

Driving away from my friend Sherry's house who lived in Sherwood Park at the time. Both girls were with me Karen was about 2 and Jess was about 4. Karen was in the government approved car seat. I didn't see it but my friend Sherry said I was tossing crackers back to Karen since she was screaming at the top of her lungs. This is Sherry's recollection.

We left Viking after a mere 3 years. Frank had asked for a raise as Town Manager, and they turned him down. He decided to look elsewhere for work, but this was not the main reason we left. I wanted to further my education and it would have been difficult to do that from Viking. One of his job searches took him to Surrey for the weekend which did not pan out, but he later found a job in Surrey, BC, as Assistant Town Clerk. We both agreed it would be a great opportunity since the salary would be better, we would be close to my family, and his family was not all that far away in Calgary. His parents did not come out to the coast all that much, but we used to go there quite often.

We had such a great time in the town of Viking, and we met some great friends, and we keep in touch with many of them, mostly on Facebook.

In fact, during the summer of 2019, we returned to Viking for Old Home Week and several of our old gang returned for the rodeo and we got to meet up with them. We had not changed, ha ha, but everyone else had. Not true. John Pullen had not really changed, just got white hair, and his wife Lynn looked as young as ever; Fred

Nordstrom and Carolyn were the same. They live in Edmonton and in the summer, they live in Viking out on the old homestead. We also saw Ed Lefsrud who is still as funny and interesting as ever. Too bad we missed his wife who was away on her 50-year nurses' reunion on the West Coast. We will connect another time for sure. I do see her periodically on Facebook.

I had wanted to return to school to study for a long time, but in the beginning, I was not sure what direction I wanted to go. I took a few courses at Douglas College in Surrey: political science and philosophy. I thought about going into law, but it did seem a little daunting as I also had the two little girls to look after. What I needed was a career that I could complete and not have a great wad of student loans to deal with afterwards.

When we moved to Surrey, we were introduced to Green Timbers Evangelical Church. This was on the recommendation of my Aunt Katherine who had visited my grandparents years ago and had attended this church. We had always gone to Anglican mainstream churches before this. In fact, the church we attended in Viking was headed by an Anglican minister, but it took place in a United Church building, and once a month, the minister would have a service in the little Anglican church in town. Strangely enough, I was asked to play the organ there once or twice, since they were desperate for someone to play at funerals. I was never all that good playing in public. I used to be asked by my dear departed grandmother to "play a tune for the guests, won't you please, Susan". I never enjoyed being put on the spot back in the day, so I guess this stayed with me but I did get a little braver as time went on. It was also an honor to be asked. She was so proud of me.

Finally, I decided to go to nurses training. I wanted to do general nursing, but there was a long wait list. The director of the nursing program, Margaret Neyland, said, however, that it would be possible for me to go to the psychiatric nurses' program, starting in August in about two weeks time. I was not sure I could pull it together in such a short time.

I was all pumped to do this, but I had to get a few things in order first, like a baby sitter for Karen and someone to provide after school care for Jessica, who was in kindergarten. We were lucky enough to be able to send her to a neighbour's who also had a daughter in in kindergarten. Karen went to the Oak Avenue Daycare and it worked out quite well. Jessica went to Marge Cutting's place as her daughter would be in the same kindergarten class and they lived right about the corner from us. I had lots of financial support since Frank was unemployed and we had no income. The government paid for the daycare totally. Luckily, we had two cars, so I drove the VW van to school.

Oh yes, my school was British Columbia Institute of Technology.

In the beginning, school was tough. I had not been in a classroom for at least 10 years, and I had two children to take to daycare, my own school, and I had to find enough money to foot the expenses for this challenge. My husband was on unemployment insurance and that was our only source of income. My parents helped a lot with picking up the girls and staying with them if Frank could not be there. I did also get some bursaries from a few non-profit agencies so that made all the difference. Frank got a job a few months later, working in West Vancouver for John Kramer, who was into property development at the time. That was a bit of a nightmare, the commute to west Vancouver, but it surely did help us.

The first clinical session in the nursing program was a medical one, and it was at St. Vincent's Hospital. I genuinely enjoyed this but getting up at 6am or earlier some mornings to avoid the traffic through the Massey Tunnel was hard. There were a few mornings I thought if I could only get pregnant then I would not have to finish this program. Then I thought what you are saying Susan, give your head a shake. So, I buckled up and got to it, and of course, I did finish.

The days I enjoyed the most at school were Wednesdays. It was the day our little clinical groupies got together and had a jam session about all the things we thought the school should change and how the instructors were doing it all wrong. The kibitzing was more fun than anything else. It was a motley group. As well, most of us were all over 30, only two were in their early 20's. I know the first day I looked around the room to see how many were as old as me, and there were quite a few. It may have been hard work, but I am truly glad I continued my journey to completion.

CHAPTER SEVENTEEN

Woodlands School for the Disabled

After I completed my nurse's training, I worked for a truly short time at Woodlands School for the mentally challenged. I worked on the unit for the younger folk who where not only mentally challenged but also had a psychiatric diagnosis. This was particularly challenging. These adults ranged in age from 20 to 40 years old chronologically but had the developmental understanding of a 4-year-old; however, they had all the urges and desires of a normal teen.

Frank had been out of work for about a year during my first year in nursing training. We had friends who had known Frank's brother David while he was working in Yellowknife a few years previously. When they moved to Surrey, they looked us up. Robin returned to Fort Smith to work as he was having such a difficult time finding stable work. Before long, Robin contacted Frank and asked him if he was interested in a job as a bookkeeper with the Town of Fort Smith. I did not think Frank would leap at the opportunity, but I had been wrong in the past. I was not all that thrilled to be uprooting again just after I had graduated and found a good job, but eventually I did succumb to the idea. It would be another journey.

So just as I was about to finish my third year and do my practicum, Frank agreed to take the job in the North. That meant that he had to leave me behind to complete my training and look after the entire ball of wax: take the kids to music lessons, pick them up from daycare, go to church, and on, and on. Well, it was going to work out fine.

My parents helped by picking up the girls when I was doing afternoon shifts at Woodlands School. I had chosen this location for my preceptorship because of the closeness to my home and how easy it would be to pick up the girls, but I needed someone to be there with them all evening when I worked late, and it was asking a little much for my folks to be on call for this. I chose to put an ad in the local newspaper for a young female to help me. I was not able to pay too much but a wonderful young lady named Tracy answered the advertisement. She would live with us and take care of the girls after school and when I needed to study. She was amazing with the girls and the two of us got along well. In fact, we are still friends to this day. When we moved to the North to join Frank in Fort Smith, she also came along. This would be her opportunity to spread her wings and fly. No pun intended but we did fly there, and she did get a job working for Buffalo Airlines.

Tracy became a part of the family for awhile. We really enjoyed having her. However, she only stayed for about a year, and then she decided she wanted to return home to her love interest on the lower mainland. We were sad to see her leave that is for sure. She had to follow her own path. We have kept in touch since we returned.

Tracy was a blessing from God. I want to say thank you to Tracy right here.

Buffalo Air *is a Northern based airline operating primarily from Yellowknife, Northwest Territories, Canada. Since 1970, Buffalo Airways has been operating as a family run business founded by Joe McBryan (aka Buffalo Joe). It operates scheduled passenger, charter passenger, charter cargo, firefighting and fuel service from out main base is at*

Yellowknife Airport (CYZF) with offices in Hay River (CYHY), a courier office in Edmonton (CYXD) and a heavy maintenance base in Red Deer (CYQF).

Graduation from nursing was a gas, especially for me. I was "single". My husband was away working in the Northwest Territories, in Fort Smith. I didn't have a date for any of the parties, so I thought who I will ask. Strangely enough, I thought "I can ask my younger brother; he is single!" I thought he looked about the same age even though he is 7 years and 10 months younger. *(He never lets me forget it either.)* He would be great, so I asked him and much to my surprise he said yes. The one big party was at The Town Pump, a restaurant, in Gas Town Vancouver. It was a dinner and dance. We even danced together. I thought it would be a great place for him to meet some new people. It did not turn out that way, but we did have a great time.

Once I got my nursing registration papers, I had a decision to make. Should I go or should I stay? Well, it would be another challenge. Frank had decided he would stay in Fort Smith, so we had to decide to make some major changes. I had to arrange to rent our house and get a mover.

Well, now I had to make the move to Fort Smith. I had to give notice for my job that I had only worked at for a few months, one I was really beginning to enjoy. I remember our pastor's wife, Anna, said to me at the going away party the ladies gave me at Green Timbers Church, "Now Susan, you are just building memories. This will not be forever."

That going-away party was one to remember. Donna Coutts, the associate pastor's wife, dressed as a wolf, supposedly to introduce us to the wildlife we would see when we got to the great White North. I had already travelled there in September to check things out and had taken the girls with me. It was probably okay and exactly what I had expected. There were no big box stores, no department stores, no movie theatres, and we still did not have a place to live except the trailer park where Frank had lived for his first 6 months. He did not have a vehicle either and had to walk to town.

We did not sell our house right away. My friend and neighbour, Esther, had a friend named Grant who needed a place to rent and he was willing to share with my brother Colin. That did not turn out well. The house became a bit of a headache after the two renters decided to move out. In fact, the house was a bit of an albatross hanging around my neck. We were so far away and keeping track of the maintenance was a chore and we did not know where we would end up living after we left the North. So, we put the house on the market. It sold very quickly, and we gratefully put the money in the bank for a rainy day. We didn't even have to move furniture out because we had taken everything with us to the NWT (Northwest Territories). I mean everything. Fort Smith was not a bad place, just literally the "end of the road". There was no where to go after you reached Fort Smith. Except maybe Pine Lake.

*The town of **Fort Smith** is in the South Slave Region of the Northwest Territories, Canada. It is in the southeastern portion of the Northwest Territories, on the Slave River and adjacent to the NWT/Alberta border. Its Chipewyan name is Thebacha meaning "beside the rapids". The community started in 1874 as a Hudson's Bay post and portage point. To get there, you have to drive north all the way up to Hay River, NWT, and then back down in a southeasterly direction to the Fort, which was remarkably close to the Saskatchewan border and near Uranium City. It was also the administrative capital of the NWT for 56 years and its population has remained at about 2,000 for many years.*

Fort Smith was a great place to work. It had a combination of doctors' offices, social services, general hospital, and long-term care facility providing medical, psychiatric, geriatric, and emergency nursing. Part of the hospital, about half, was for permanent patients and an extended care facility. The remainder was an acute care facility There were 36 general duty beds. Families visited regularly and often brought traditional food of the native culture with them.

The hospital had never had a psychiatric nurse working for them so my training was a great asset for the hospital and I was asked to talk to different patients with psychiatric concerns.

We lived in a trailer park for the first week we were there and then moved to a lovely home that the town mayor owned. It was a nice place until the mayor decided he had a sale for the home and we had to pack up again and move to the empty church manse.

Nursing in the North was an interesting job since I got to use all of my medical skills. I was trained primarily as a psychiatric nurse, and the person who interviewed me wanted me to be able to use my psychiatric skills as well. These skills allowed me to support people who were grieving or had personal problems. Some people just needed someone to listen to them and they did not always get that. At night around 8 pm, the doors were all locked and if an emergency doctor was needed, you had to ring the buzzer. This was a good thing because otherwise everyone would be coming through the door wanting a hand out of an aspirin or anything from soup to nuts. One peculiar thing happened about 19.45 pm most Wednesday nights. A few families came in with their children to have them admitted for dysentery so they could go to the Bingo at the Catholic church. We had a few extra babies occasionally. Difficult to get around that.

At one point, I applied for a job as an alcohol and drug counsellor with the First Nations. I had to go through a panel interview with local band members. I was quite sure I would get the job, but the successful candidate was an alcoholic, not in recovery, and the big deal was that I was neither local nor a long-time resident. When I was not getting many hours at the hospital, I was offered another opportunity. This time it was working with the Continuing Education program and helping people without high school qualifications get the assistance they were unable to get in the local school. Most of them were older students. This was a great experience to renew my old math skills. I just continued working at the Health Center as it was called until we left the North.

I hadn't actually seen a dead person since completing nursing school, but it wasn't long before I got my opportunity. "Mr. Smith", a patient, was well aware that he was going to pass away soon, and he had waited for all his family members to arrive and in order to say his goodbyes.

Mr. Smith's last son arrived from the East Coast of Canada, just in time for him to say his good-byes. The next process was to prepare his body and take it to the morgue. The preparations went fine, but when the nursing staff got to the morgue, they had to slip his body into a drawer. The drawer opened sideways, not like the ones you see in CSI Miami where the first thing you see when the drawer is the head. Well, it took a team effort to arrange the body for sure. What made it even more macabre was that it happened in the middle of the night. We lifted his body onto the tray on the bottom shelf and ever so gently placed it in the metal cupboard, but my foot was stuck under Mr. Smith. I gasped and screamed, "HELP", but the scream was almost inaudible for anyone else. I did not want to be left in the drawer too. It became a little comical actually and everyone started to laugh. A couple of them fell on the floor in laughter and then got on their knees and positioned Mr. Smith correctly before quickly shoving him in place and shutting the drawer. The laughter was nervous laughter. It really was a serious job we were doing, but the laughter helped us get through the ordeal.

We had some fantastic times in the North. There were lots of social activities. Every spring meant a well-attended steak and lobster party. There was a group of people in town who were all from the Maritimes and there was a group from the province of Newfoundland.

We bought cross country skis on our way North to Fort Smith and we planned to get involved in winter activities. The girls and every one got involved as well. What was great about this sport was that even though we lived on the main street, we could put on our skis and gear and leave right from the house. At the cross-country ski chalet, hot chocolate or hot lemonade were available always. That hot drink was much appreciated.

Once while we lived there, the three of us flew back from Edmonton to Fort Smith, my seat number was called and I won a dog sled ride back to town. I chose not to use the win but gave it to the girls. Jessica chose to take the ride into town.

We made sure we took in all the great sights before we left the North. One of these was to go on a buffalo hunt. We also wanted to ride the river raft tour on the Great Slave Lake. This was truly a highlight since I have always been a scaredy-cat when it comes to water. We stopped halfway through the trip, got off the rafts, and sat on the rocks where we were treated to a picnic lunch with white wine in fancy plastic glasses. Jack Van Pelt was the tour guide. He had been born in Helmond, the Netherlands, moved to Canada in 1954, and attended McGill University where he met his first wife, Mary. In 1969, he attended Michigan State University and met his second wife, Ruth.

Jack Van Pelt, *an environmentalist, made many trips up and down the Mackenzie River in the 1960s. Among his other jobs, he started a Fort Smith-based ecotourism business named Subarctic Wilderness Adventures. The business connected people from across the world with locals in the NWT. Before he died, he wrote, "I will return to nature from which I was born, highly favoured," (Wikipedia)*

You really had to decide to make the best of life while you were there. It took a while to get a job at the hospital, but I managed to find part time work there. One of the highlights of working at the hospital in Fort Smith was getting to fly patients out of town to a bigger hospital. My turn for this adventure did not come for quite awhile, at least it felt like that. When it did happen, it was Oct. 31st, the one night I wanted to be with the girls for trick or treating. I had to escort a male patient to the Psychiatric Unit at the University of Alberta Hospital in Edmonton. It was all interesting for me. We were on a Pacific Western Airlines flight and the patient was right beside me, but the three seats in front and three seats behind us were blocked off. He was apparently a risk for mood and behavior changes. It all went well.

After the patient was safely in the hands of the U of A hospital staff, I was taken to the Four Seasons Hotel in downtown Edmonton. The poshness of the hotel was fabulous! I got a stocked mini-bar and it was still stocked when I left the next day. So, what was the perk? The perk was the hotel stay itself and getting to shop in the big city of Edmonton. I felt so special. On other occasion, I had to go to Fort McMurray to drop off a pregnant patient who would have been at risk had she stayed in Fort MacMurray. Then there were other times I went to Yellowknife for patients. I was a flying nurse.

One flight was on a six-passenger plane from which all the seats on one sided had been removed, making room for the ailing patient's stretcher. The flight was only to Edmonton. On a jet plane, it would have taken about two hours. Well, this one took 8 hours, and the plane shook and rattled the entire way. I will never forget that flight. The patient was vomiting all the way and the family member had a plastic bag attached to his face too. Good thing nurses have strong stomachs, not all though.

The house we finally settled into in Fort Smith was one of the vacant houses, originally rented by a teacher. It was right beside the school. Great location for our daughters. They literally just had to roll out of bed, get dressed, and walk about 100 steps to the front door of the school. We stayed in this house for two years until we decided to leave the north country and return to the lower mainland. That house holds a lot of memories for sure. We decorated a little and put wallpaper in the front room that looked like bamboo reeds. We had several great Christmas celebrations there and we even had my parents' 35th wedding anniversary there.

One Sunday singing in church so loud to let others hear me, not that I had a great voice, but I enjoyed singing hymns. one daughter on either side of me and the older of the two said Mom stop singing my ears are bleeding.

The most shocking thing I remember about this house was the living room on the second floor. You say why would this be remarkable. Well, for one thing, you could just sit up there on the sofa and look down on the world. One day I was sitting looking out and a few kids were playing in the street. Then they brought out an area rug and one of the kids lay down in the middle and the others rolled him into it. Next, I was shocked to see that they started to roll him down the street. I jumped up, opened the sliding window, and screamed from the top of my lungs. "GET OFF THE ROAD". At first, they did not do a thing. Then they jumped up when they realized there was a car heading right toward them. I am sure the car would have stopped but one will never know. I think if I had been looking out a main floor window that day I would have run out and scolded the kids but opening the window and yelling like a street urchin was a better way to spark the kids to move to safety.

I have always been one to react quickly and have a plan for recovery. I am not sure where that comes from. Even when I was working in the more stressful of times in the psychiatric unit, I was able to diffuse difficult situation. I have been told I have a calming presence. Well, I will take that as a compliment. We must take them when they come along.

We loved the northern life but there came a point when we thought we needed to move back to the West Coast to be closer to our families and where there would be more work opportunity for me. So, that is what the family did. Frank gave his resignation to the town and I looked for places to live in the White Rock/South Surrey area. we saved our nest egg from selling our little bi-level on Linton Way. I still remember that house number, 13108. It is still there but you would never in a million years recognize it. The new people have totally renovated it, put on an addition, and an attached garage. The only thing we had had done was to fix up the basement.

We arranged our move for the end of the school year and rented a Ryder truck. This was another experience. The darn truck broke down before we even got to take it to Fort Smith to load it up for the long drive back south to Surrey. Finally, the truck was loaded and we were "on the road again". In Hay River, the truck broke down again! That did not go well. Now there is not a lot to do in Hay River even though it is known as "the Hub of the North".

Hay River is located in the Northwest Territories on the south shore of the Great Slave Lake at the mouth of the Hay River. The town is

separated into two sections: New Town and Old Town with the Hay River/Merlyn Airport between them. Hay River along with Fort Smith are the two regional centres for the South Slave Region.

CHAPTER EIGHTEEN

Family History

I think this is a good time to tell you a bit about my family background, where I came from genetically or hereditarily-speaking. I strongly believe that people are who they are because of many things and that we can change many of the outcomes in our lives for sure. We can change the factors contributing to our health, the ones that so determine our strength and our capacity for life in general. So many of us think, "Well, my mother or my father had a heart condition that was lethal and so I will have the same condition too. Or my mother had COPD because she smoked too much". But it does not always have to turn out that way. We can all alter our path, somewhat. We may all be brought up right, whatever that is, but for some people it goes fine but for others not so fine.

I will start with my mother. Unfortunately for us, she passed away about a year ago and we all miss her dearly, especially my Dad. She was born in Prince Albert, Saskatchewan, and she was an only child. Her father had immigrated from Britain when he was in his late 20's and the family had pioneered land there. Her mother was born in Nova Scotia, the youngest of 8 children. When her mother died, she was only about 2 years old. Her father raised all 8 children and figured out a way create enough income to provide for them. He had no family support at all and his only choice was to leave them alone all day long while he went out and fished for their living. That only worked for awhile though. My Dad tells of a story about when my great grandfather was away fishing, and the children were at home alone. They had a few sheep on their property and for entertainment they hog tied one of the sheep and used the poor little thing as a trampoline.

My grandmother told us the story of how one day when her father was away fishing, all the children decided that entire family should travel by train all the way to Prince Albert in northern Saskatchewan where other family members lived and where they could find someone able to help with all these children. All the older children lived with their father while the two younger girls, Aunt May, and my grandmother, were sent to live with a good friend of the family, Geddes Mitchel and his wife, Ida. The two girls stayed there most of their lives. My grandmother was never adopted by this couple but later they became known as my great grandparents. I guess you see where this is going. My auntie was probably asked to return to her father's residence to cook and clean for her other siblings so as a result, she had to leave school. This was a common occurrence back in the early 1900's. Then as time went by, my grandmother left school to look after my great grandmother and so did not complete her high school either. She later met Oscar, my grand father. There was 15 years difference in their ages. So, this is the brief scenario of the grandparents.

My brother never considered the "great grandparents" as family because they were not blood related. I sometimes feel that family does not have to be blood.

My grandfather owned a grocery store and my mother had to work in the store. She loved waiting on customers. In fact, she would rush home after school and work at the store rather than do homework. When she was only 13 years old, she travelled by train all the way to Nova Scotia where my great grandparents lived on a small farm. There she attended grade 7 or 8. I am not sure which or just how old she was at that time. She enjoyed her year away, but when it came time for the next school year to start, her mother, my grandmother, travelled all the way to Nova Scotia by train and took her back with her. She experienced a lot of turmoil with the moving, travelling, and different school curriculum. Not just that, but she was missing the friend connection.

These are crucial times in any teenager's life. She only managed to continue in school until the end of grade 9 and then opted to enroll in a business college in Prince Albert. She was successful and started working immediately after she completed the course at Western Grocery supplier. As it happened, this business was one of the suppliers for my grandfather's grocery. She always resented the fact that she felt she had had to take this job because of the connection. Shortly afterwards, she and her family sold the grocery store and packed up everything they owned and moved to Nova Scotia to be near her grandparents (Ida and Geddes Mitchel). My grandfather was horrified when he found out where they would be located. My great grandfather lived in the back of beyond, a place called Jordan Ferry. There was no work for him unless he got himself a car and worked in Shelburne, Nova Scotia.

Jordan Ferry *is a community in the Shelburne County, Nova Scotia, a dirt road and no town anywhere near by. It is located along the southeastern coast of Nova Scotia on the west side of Jordan Bay almost at the end of a long peninsula. The nearest town is Shelburne.*

Soon after they arrived, my great grandfather offered my grandfather a piece of land across the road from his property so he could build his own place on. Apparently, this triggered in him the thought, "I got to get out of here" because they moved to Dartmouth, across the harbour from Halifax where he eventually found a job at a local grocery store. At that time, it was known as the DOMINION STORE. He worked there for awhile until he found an opportunity to work at Cousins" Dry Cleaners. This suited him well as he had been trained in England as a tailor, and he certainly had a special talent in that field.

I loved him dearly, but it is my mother's story I want to concentrate on here. She was so special, and she dedicated her life, while she was still single, to her mother and father. They were a threesome, which is interesting. My father's sister had married Ludwick Zedbiak and they too had only one daughter. They, too, were a threesome. An unusual thing about the Zebiaks was they had three of everything in their house. Cups, chairs, plates, knives, and forks. They very rarely, if ever, had guests in their home.

My mother met my father while she was working at the Chronicle Herald in Halifax. They were married about 5 months later, and their marriage lasted 71 plus years. She was a dedicated woman in her own right. She was noticeably quiet, but she did have a temper, more out of frustration than any thing. She sometimes did not know what to do with either my brother or me and so would let it slide and not address the issue. I think that is perhaps how she was raised. She used to say sometimes that there were many things she wished she had done when she was growing up but often said, "You don't speak up in our family, at least not with my father. It just is not done. You do not cross him or question anything he says". So, she grew up in a loving home, but no one spoke ever out in opposition. Don't get me wrong, my Grandfather Oscar was a lovely man and loved us dearly, but he was quietly stern. I think that is lay terms' stubborn.

My grandfather was certainly quiet and kind but stubborn, or at least had firm beliefs. My mother had some of those too. She was very stubborn too when it came to me and what I was to do. I did not think any thing of it at the time. I never questioned anything either.

Just a memory.

I remember one time when I was about 9 years old, we were living at 72 Micmac Street. My mother sent me to the store about 5 blocks away for a loaf of bread. Well, of course, I did what she asked. I got the bread and headed home but very shortly after I started home it begam to pour rain just as I was coming to a schoolmate's,

Michael Coolen's house. I ran up to the door to get out of the storm and I stayed until it stopped raining. Then they gave me a bag for the bread, and I headed home. When I got home my mother was trembling and asked in a stern voice, "Where were you? What has happened to the bread?" The original paper bag had disintegrated in the rain before I got to my friend's house, but my mother was livid. I started to get really scared so I ran for my bedroom and hid under the bed. I had an old hospital bed with tubed framing, and it was high off the floor. I stayed under there for awhile and when I thought it was safe, I came out. She had calmed down. There was only one other time I remember her losing her cool with me. It was when I revealed my final marks from my first year in grade 12 and she lit into me! Oh my gosh! I could not believe it!

My mother overall was a calm person who did not say much to anyone that would upset them. She did tell me many times she thought she would like to speak up to my Dad, but she knew her voice would not be heard. She was such a caring person who would do anything for anyone. She had a big heart for such a little lady. As an adult, I towered over her. She always wore about a size 2 dress and I am a size12. My height is my fathers' contribution. He is a big man.

My mother worked full time when I was a little girl up until my brother was born and then my grandmother Ella became my babysitter. That worked out well.

A funny thing happened one day while she was babysitting. I was playing with the neighborhood kids and we were running all over the place playing some sort of a game. One kid tried to stop them by tossing a small rock to catch the group's attention. Lo and behold, didn't the rock go flying into the window of the corner pharmacy. The huge window crashed ...boom... bang. All the other kids ran for the hills and I was left behind running for my grandmother's house. I was the only one that the pharmacist saw. So, when I got back to grandma's house, I was huffing a puffing. A few minutes later, there came a knock on the door. Grandma opened the door and there was a police officer asking to talk to me. A poor little waif … only 5 years old. I told grandma and she started to scold me, and I piped up, "I will tell Tom." That was a line I used to use when I was being scolded by Grandma. I loved my grandma. To this day I still wish I could go see her and have tea. I do hope she is preparing a place at the table for me.

After my brother was born, my mother didn't work again until I was married, and our oldest daughter was 12 months old. Then, she went to work at Woodward's, a department store which does not exist anymore. Mother worked there until she was 65 and she was determined to get the discount pass when she retired. She loved her job. It was her great chance for independence, that is for sure.

Mom made new friends there, and after she retired, she kept in touch with some from the store. Woodward's has since been sold to the Hudson Bay Corporation but even after that she retained her discount. My Dad was so insulted after Mom passed that he was not able to keep the Mom's employee discount.

I guess in many ways, I am very much like my mother and that is not a bad thing for sure. She was always getting new ideas and wanting to do new things. She wanted me to get more education even after I had my nursing diploma. "Oh, get your Master's," she said. So, I did get my Master's' but not in nursing.

I felt I wanted to branch out into other areas. So, it was A's in Theology that I got, and then I thought I should get my PhD. So, I did and finished that about a year before mom passed. I was glad that I had done it so she was able to see my success. I was awfully close to mom. We went to Red Hats, a women's organization, sometimes. It was more for her than me, but the ladies were lovely to me and mom she was the original "Queen Mom" in her group. (The original group was a Coronation Street fan club but later they opted to call themselves The Coronation Red Hatters.) Later they handed that honor over to Wendy Taylor (no relationship but we did call her "cousin" but only because of the same last name.) After that, mom became the Baroness. I must admit I always wanted to please my mom. I hope I did her proud. This is a little picture of my mom.

Now then, a little about my father. My Dad is a different force of nature. I always loved my Dad and respected him but really in the same breath I must say that I was a little in awe of his presence. He was so big, and he was clearly the one in control. I never wanted to ask him anything. He did not usually listen to me, so I thought. If I had something to say, I would ask my mother instead. My Dad is a big imposing figure not that he was someone to be feared but being a little girl, he towered over my little mother and me. He had two older sisters, but he was the favorite for sure. His mother once told him that if he had been born first, she would not have had anymore children. That was a difficult pill to swallow. I cannot imagine a mother saying that to her son especially when there were already two older sisters. He had a very close relationship with his mother. He spent a lot of time with his Mom and Dad, travelling on his summer vacations mostly to Boston to see family friends. He tells a lovely story about one of the trips to Boston when his mother, Mrs. Vowinkle, and another friend went on their own on a train trip. While they were there, they bought him a lovely leather bag with a handle and straps. He wore it to school and the kids would bully him mostly because they were jealous. His Dad was always a little suspicious of Mrs. Vowinkle as he thought she was a German spy. She treated him extra special. She always had new cars.

There is one very strange thing, well, I think it is. We never met our grandparents on my Dad's side of the family. Only ever saw my grandmother and grandfather once, and that was from a distance and from the inside the car. He was on the steps of his home in Enfield. I asked Dad once why we never got invited to their house. He was a little surprised I think that I had asked but he just passed it off saying, "Oh well, that is the way it was." I cannot imagine not spending time with my grandparents and why would they not want to see their grandchildren? We will never know the truth. I am so glad I got to know my grandparents on my mother's side and that my children did also.

Dad always told me he never went any further than Grade Two. I know this is not true since he went to St. Ann's school in Church Point, Nova Scotia and after that he went to King's College. His sisters did not go to private school though.

He left home about the time that he got a job selling advertising for the Halifax Chronicle Herald. This was where he met my mother who was the receptionist and secretary there. They did not start dating until after he left that job. He loved to tell the story of how he got his long-time job at Pilkington Glass, a job he loved until he retired.

After Mom and Dad retired, Mom had a dream of having a teddy bear shop and Dad wanted to be a balloon man, so the two of them created a balloon and party shop. The entire family got involved: we stocked the store with wonderful teddy bears and plush animals too. There were giraffes, ducks, and elephants. It was such a great place to be. We decorated the small store and hung wallpaper that was rainbows and clouds.

That was a time when we all worked together. My brother Colin and I did something together and we had fun. We dressed up in theme costumes and delivered helium balloons to parties all over the White Rock area. We both did clown costumes, but he did have better costumes. I was once asked to deliver in a Raggedy Ann costume and to sing in French to an exceptionally large wedding party in someone's garden. This did go amazingly well for someone who had extremely poor French pronunciation, but I did manage to pull off Frère Jacques. I only had to sing it about three times. Colin sometimes dressed as the Grim Reaper for 40th birthday parties. I think the most embarrassing time for me was when I had to go to the local hospital where I also worked as a nurse, dressed in the Raggedy Ann costume. Of course, I ran into my head nurse, Elaine Hall, coming down the stairs as I was travelling up. We had a good laugh over this.

Dad was in his element at the party store. He was, and is, such a social butterfly. The most hilarious memory of my Dad and Frank comes from when they were delivering a bouquet of balloons to this very posh home on an acreage near White Rock. Dad and Frank went together and that was a good thing because, I am sure, they would have had to pick Dad up off the floor. They very innocently knocked at the front door. A few seconds went by, and oh my, the door opened and standing before them was a very lovely woman with a martini in her hand and wearing nothing else. They apparently were ushered into the house to present the bouquet to the birthday girl. They high tailed it out of there real fast.

Delivering balloons to a wedding in a backyard dressed in a Raggedy Ann costume. I had to sing Frere Jacques in French. I had to sing three times so maybe this makes me bilingual. This was when we had the balloon and party store "Cuddlies & Co".

Oh yes, there's another time I must mention for sure. They both delivered to the Old Beach Hotel, on Marine Drive, to the Main Act. It was a strip joint. When they walked in, there was Missy Blue

Eyes slithering on the stage. You sure could not see her eyes or how blue they were ... and she was the one who was reaching the balloons. They were so embarrassed. I am sure these two men never moved so fast after the delivery. Who said delivering balloons was a risqué job? Who would have thought? Not me!

Dad can charm the ear off an aardvark. The balloon shop did not last too long, but we did have a great time. Dad, we love you. Oh, and my mom was also working at Woodward's at the same time. Often, she would rush to Woodward's after working in the balloon shop. They were both so social. We love you, Mom.

A few little nuggets that my Dad still loves to tell.

My Dad had only dated my mother three times when, he says, he knew then that he wanted to marry her. So, when he asked her to marry him, she said "Tom just slow down, don't be in such a hurry."

When they were living in Peterborough, he was working at a brick yard and the owner gave my Dad two tickets for the drive-in movies. He thanked the owner very much but told him that he didn't have a car. The owner said, "No problem Tom, you can use the dump truck. So, this is what they did. Then they got to the drive-in, they had to park right at the back parking lot so the truck wouldn't block the view.

When my parents returned from Peterborough to Halifax in the spring before I was born, my Dad needed a job. He tells it like this. "I have your mother to thank for the job I got at Pilkington Glass". She saw the ad in the Halifax chronicle newspaper and sent in a letter applying for the job. Then I got the call from the Human Resources for an interview." He obviously got the job, but he says he would never have got the job if it was not for my mother.

Here's another tale. My parents were driving with my grandparents in my mother's new car on their way from Edmonton to our place in Viking. Well, on the way, they were hit head on by a car going extremely fast. It was my mother's brand-new station wagon. Mom was blown away. She jumped out of the car and ran up the man who had hit them. Apparently, she grabbed him by the lapels and started to shake him back and forth. "Why did you hit my new car?" The other driver said as she was shaking him, "I never hit a woman!" The driver had a burning cigarette dangling from his lips during the whole episode. Since the passing of my mom a few years ago he tells this story over and over again I think just to show how tough she was and a stressful situation. She really was a strong lady.

CHAPTER NINETEEN

The Piano

We became heir to the family piano, a travelling piano. It had journeyed across the country many times before we finally became the lawful owners of the old Heinzman. Eventually it ended up in Fort Chippewan, NWT (Northwest Territories) when we sold it prior to returning to the lower mainland from Fort Smith.

Here is our piano story.

This story and the piano started in Prince Albert, Saskatchewan. From there, it travelled to Halifax, Nova Scotia, Then, it moved along with my father when he was transferred from Halifax to Saint John, New Brunswick, and from there it went to Edmonton, Alberta.

I did not have my own piano until we moved to Viking from Edmonton. The family piano was left in my mother's house in, Edmonton, Alberta. She said I could have it so I could teach basic and beginner's piano lessons. When Frank and I got married in 1972, I took the piano with me to Viking, Alberta and later to Surrey, BC. and then on to Fort Smith, NWT. Now it is in Fort Simpson in the Northwest Territories. It was hard to decide to sell it but transporting it when we moved south would have been very costly. I took the money from the sale though and bought a new one when we arrived in Surrey. We had already moved it three times. If only that old piano could talk. Something like the story of the traveling pants, a move from the past.

We had built a lovely house in Viking, but we did not know exactly where we would place the dear old piano; however, when we fixed up the basement so the girls and their friends could play down there, the piano had a home. We painted the floor of the basement bright shiny red. What a great difference that made. It was a fun place to go. There was a shag rug on the floor. Not long after the decorating was complete, the travelling piano came. It was a great addition, and then Frank's parents gave us their green piano when they moved into a luxury high rise and had no place for it. So, for a short while we had two pianos. Memory does not serve me well here as I do not know what prompted us to take both pianos. It was very funky when I reflect on it now. I guess I felt we should take something that came from Frank's family home, but a piano? It was like taking an elephant and it was as difficult to move.

The interesting thing about the honkytonk green piano was that when we decided to remove the green color, we discovered a beautiful piano made from teak and mahogany. We only kept the two pianos for a brief time though and sold the green one to our neighbour to the east of our house So much for the green piano.

Once we were established in Viking, I needed something to do so I started to teach beginner piano lessons. My first two students were the two Kripps boys. They were so adorable, but one was far more interested in learning to play the instrument than the other. They came once a week and progressed very well. I had about 6 students from the local areas. It was a great challenge since both our girls were quite little and needed attention at times, but I usually managed to have Karen, our youngest, napping when the students came over. Jessica was always keen to find something to do or she would go over to the Watson's house and play around with Sara.

Our dear friend John Pullen had an insurance agency in town, and he approached me asking if I would like to work for him one day a week in his office. I suspect it was his way of saying, "Hey Susan, you need to get out of the house". I was with the girls all the time and certainly needed a change. My parents lived in Edmonton, so I also needed to find someone to look after my two beauties while I worked. I managed to find a Mrs. Ratray who was a grandmother type, and she was perfect. They did not make strange, and I did not feel guilty leaving them. It did take me a couple of days to get over the fact that I was leaving them, but it was good for them too. I was able to work a little and go out for lunch periodically and then go home. Then, the family felt all new and ready for me for another week. Once a week was good.

The travelling piano came with us for the years we lived in Fort Smith. It was way too much travelling for my great grandfather's old piano to move again and costly to transport, so we sold it to a young couple who lived in Fort Simpson, Northwest Territories. We took the money we got from the sale and bought the piano we now have. With the new piano, we got six weeks of lessons, so Frank took the lessons. Today that piano is still with us here in Boundary Creek, New Brunswick. When we first moved here to New Brunswick I took some lessons to brush up on my playing. It still needs a lot of work.

When we left Fort Smith, the moving truck held everything we owned, even my motor scooter but no piano.

The scooter was a bit of a pipe dream it was great while we lived in Fort Smith there was no traffic to speak of. So I would drive it around town and to work at the hospital. I was able to park it in the ambulance bay when I worked the night shift.

My brother had agreed to fly to Fort Smith (we paid his flight) in order to drive our van to BC while Frank drove the rental truck. My job was to run interference with the girls in the two vehicles. Our ride south was extremely eventful.

We were ready to leave the North and head for BC. Everything was on the rented Ryder truck but early in our trip, the rental truck broke down in Hay River, NWT. After it was fixed, we were finally ready to head south and west to Vancouver and then on to White Rock. Colin and I and Jess, our daughter, were ahead of Frank and Karen, our second daughter. They had quite a load as they were towing our 1974 Volvo behind the rental truck. We did not realize that they were stopped by the side of the road in the Fraser Canyon because the truck had broken down again. This time our Volvo just was just barely hanging onto the edge of the shoulder of the road. Frank took Karen, who was only 7 years old at the time, and headed for a pay phone to get help. They hitchhiked a long way back to the last town. Eventually, the truck and the car were both towed to our new rental house in South Surrey.

When the three of us arrived in White Rock at my parents' house, we were welcomed with open arms and everyone was keen to find out all about our trip, but where were Karen and Frank. We had not seen them in our travels. We must have passed them and thought they would catch up, but they never did. We were also greeted by Cousin Maxine and Ken so the house was full. My granny loved it when all the family were there, laughing and telling stories. The three of us were glad to have arrived, but exhausted. I so loved my grandmother. I still wish she were here but that is impossible. She is with the angels.

That night, we had just sat down to supper when the phone rang. It was Frank calling to say they were in Boston Bar, in the Fraser Canyon, and that the Ryder Truck had broken down and he and Karen would have to take a bus to White Rock.

Boston Bar: *The name dates from the time of the Fraser Canyon Gold Rush (1858–1861). A "bar" is a gold-bearing sandbar or sandy riverbank, and the one slightly down river and opposite today's town was populated heavily by Americans, who were known in the parlance of the Chinook Jargon as "Boston men" or simply "Boston's". A settlement developed on the east bank of the river to the north of the confluence with Anderson River. This was later moved to the present site with the construction of Canadian Northern Pacific Railway.*

*The original Thompsons Salis name for Boston Bar was rendered in English-style spelling as **Quayome**, which appears commonly on frontier-era maps and in diaries and newspapers of the day. The name originally referred to the other side of the river from today's town but came into use for the present site after the original was renamed North Bend by the Canadian Pacific Railway.*

In June 2011, Boston Bar briefly unofficially changed its name to "Vancouver Bar", to support the nearby NHL Vancouver Canucks hockey team in the Stanley Cup Finals as they took on the Boston Bruins. This follows major retailers such as Boston Pizza unofficially changing their name to "Vancouver Pizza" during the same round of the playoffs.

Frank and Karen did not arrive until much later that night. The Ryder truck with all our furniture did not arrive until the next day. Until it did, we conjured up many ideas of how and what had happened to the Volvo that had been attached to the moving truck. It was left parked on the edge of the cliff near Boston Bar attached to the Ryder Truck. What a trip. We are very thankful for all the help my brother contributed to get the van back to the west coast.

1987

The story about Herb.

Frank at this time was out of work and found an opportunity to go into business with a known crook, but this man was what you would call a "wolf in sheep's clothing". Herb Engelbrecht came to Frank and asked him to do the finances for him, telling Frank a sad story, and using the line "I am a Christian. You can trust me". I never tend to trust someone who must tell you they are a Christian for validity. He absconded with a lot of Frank's money and put our house on the line too.

Here is how it happened.

Herb had neglected to pay Workmen's Compensation and Unemployment Insurance for his business as he was supposed to do. Frank was the bookkeeper at the time the reports were falsified and so we were held responsible. Just at this time, we had planned a family trip to Europe, so Frank had arranged for his brother David to co-sign a bank loan for Herb using our house as collateral as well as having given him a large sum of money.

A short time after giving him the money, which we never saw again, Herb locked Frank out of the office. Frank was literally conned out of a large sum of money by this man and we ended up on the government books as owing them a lot of money. We kept asking why they were not going after Herb but they said they could not find him. It turned out everything was in his wife's name. Somehow Herb got away with it.

The saddest part of this money "exchange" was that we tried to get our money back for years but finally we had to declare bankruptcy in order to get out from under the government debt load.

I did not know anything about this until years later. There were a lot of times when Frank did not tell me what was going on. That was the way he was taught, I think. "Don't tell your wife everything". My father did not always discuss everything with my mother either.

We could never locate Herb again until years later when we were sitting in a café in Fort Langley, BC. I looked to the end of the table and saw his wife sitting there and he was next to her. I thought, "I know those people" and of course it was Herb. I was truly kind and pleasant and didn't say much except "hello". A few minutes later, they got up and quickly left. I always felt betrayed about not being part of Frank's plan. He did not share anything with me at that time in our lives.

CHAPTER TWENTY

Woodland's Continued

When we returned to White Rock in British Columbia from Fort Smith, I had to get a job, so Frank and I went on a job-hunting excursion to Woodlands School for the Mentally Challenged. This Woodlands School no longer exists but here is a little history about it.

It was established on the New Westminster cricket pitch in 1878. This Public Hospital for the Insane was a castle-like fortress overlooking the B.C. Penitentiary and the Fraser River. In 1950, the B.C. government, which ran the facility, decided to separate disabled children from the adult lunatics (we would certainly not say lunatic today. We are more politically correct than that.) These adults were sent to Essondale, and the institution was renamed Woodlands School. Woodlands became home to the province's unwanted kids. The list of residents included babies abandoned at birth in a hospital, the hyperactive, the epileptic, the intellectually challenged, the disabled, children who were wards of the court, and children displaced by the closure of Vancouver's orphanage. They all lived within Woodlands' walls and cottages.

When we drove up to Woodlands School, I thought maybe I would get a job there, just maybe. We had only been back from the North for about 3 days, but I thought it was time to start looking again.

I had been there before, about three years previously, to do my third-year preceptorship for the Psychiatric Nursing Program from BCIT so I did have some knowledge of the place. I remembered working here in the summer during college and the first time I walked onto Unit 60 I found the patients were profoundly challenged. Everyone, including the staff, were all sitting down around the perimeter of the day room. I was a little uneasy at first because I could not tell who staff were and who were residents. Finally, someone stood up and I was relieved to see someone "normal".

When I walked through the door that day in the summer of 1984 and asked if there were any openings, Joan Bond, the Director, literally grabbed me by the hand and said "Come here, we are desperate and you can start tomorrow". That was the quickest hire in all the history of job searching that I could have imagined. It was not a dream job but someone had to do it. When I went back to the car where Frank was waiting, he was astounded at how quickly I had gotten a job.

The facility provided uniforms so that was a bonus right off. The worst part of the job was that when we had to change the diapers on these poor darlings who did not have a care in the world, we were required to measure it (the bowel movement) and describe its color and quantity. What a delightful job. We surely were not paid enough to do this.

Here is another example of me not speaking up for myself. There was a drug error made and it was blamed on a new nurse. Neither she nor I had the guts to speak up and say, "It wasn't me." Well, it was not me who made the mistake but I saw a pattern developing and so I started to pursue a job elsewhere. I had had enough of working with the mentally challenged, who in those days when I was in training were called "retarded" That certainly sounds horrible now. What I really wanted was to work with individuals who were mentally ill and use the skills, I had learned, to help them.

I applied at Surrey Memorial Hospital (SMH) and was successful in getting a place on the Inpatient Unit as a casual nurse. Soon after it became permanent. The patients on Unit 2E were there because they were suicidal, psychotic, depressed, or just had a bad experience with drugs, resulting in psychotic episodes. The wide range of diagnoses I experienced there was helpful to me as a "new" grad. Well, it was about 4 years after my actual graduation, but the first two and half of those years were spent in a general hospital in Fort Smith. It was definitely a big change. This was a great learning curve for my career.

There was also opportunity to assist in electro-convulsive therapy for those patients who had persistent thoughts and just needed that little nudge to push them away from those repetitive thoughts, those nagging evil thoughts. Some would say this form of treatment was barbaric, but it does have a place and today its implementation is far less barbaric with patients being closely monitored before and after the treatment. There have been great strides made with this form of therapy. Now I would not want to have it myself, even though I have had nagging and persevering thoughts that I just could not get out of my head too but that is not the same at all. Or is it?

While working at SMH, I did mostly night shift so I could be home with our girls. Well, I would be home to help them get off to school and when I woke up at about 3.30 in the afternoon they were just coming home from school. Frank was working in West Vancouver for John Kramer, although I am not sure what he did there. It was a good set up and the girls were never alone. When I reflect on those days, I remember coming home to find my kitchen sink filled with pots and pans that had been used to make Kraft dinner when Jessica and her friends descended on the house, making themselves at home. I was happy they did this, not because of the mess but because I knew where the girls were. Karen, on the other hand, did not always bring her friends home after school. She usually went to her friend Emily's place in Ocean Park.

During the night shift at SMH, it was incredibly difficult to stay awake some nights even though we had to make 15-minute and 30-minute checks depending on the severity of the patient's condition. Some nights we took our breaks and slept in the visitors' lounge for an hour. Other nights, we just stayed in the nursing station, nodding our heads to stay awake. One of the nurses I worked for, Virgilio, used to do crafts in the back alcove and would make covers for hangers. He has since passed, but he did manage to keep busy and made many covered hangers. The things we remember about people is remarkable sometimes. He was a nice man and he meant but he had this constant sniffle, and it was irritating to work nights with him. He did not work any other shift with this constant annoying sound, and he did it all night long. After a while, you just did not hear it until it was really quiet, and then there it was again. I like to think that I don't do that.

Surrey Memorial was a great experience, but I always felt I was being passed over for various opportunities on the unit. There was one nurse I felt was the favorite and she thought she was the best. That was alright except I had not learned yet that you have to speak up to get anywhere in life.

The Inpatient Unit at Surrey Memorial Hospital is where I met many of my now close friends, with whom I still keep in touch to this very day. They have remained close and we even get to socialize too. The best part during the 2020 Pandemic was Lucy Taylor who now lives in Washington State. She would arrange Zoom get-togethers. Kudos to Lucy.

There were many nurses at SMH who had finished their training a year before or after me. We all grew in knowledge together, a great learning curve. This was not at all like Woodlands School. There are still a group of us whom we refer to as the Movie Stars that are connected. We are nurses social workers admin staff and other medical disciplines.

I was getting tired of night shift, and I decided to resign and do some other kind of nursing in the community, so I applied to work part-time at the Evergreen Baptist Nursing Home. At the same time, we were involved with my Dad's party store which meant delivering balloons for various occasions across the area. This was a good thing since it made it possible for me to keep a closer watch on our youngest daughter, Karen, who was a formidable force in everyone's life. Sometimes I would get a call from the school that Karen was having problems so I could just leave and sort things out. She never did run away though. She was just more vocal than most. She was not as horrible as the teachers made out. It was only her Principal at H.D. Thrift Elementary. Karen was and is an extraordinarily strong individual. She was exceedingly high energy and always wanted a challenge in her life. That still has not changed and that is wonderful, especially for her own daughter too.

While working at the Evergreen Nursing Home, I also had a part time job at the White Rock Come Share, an Adult Day Care for seniors who needed socialization. Some even just needed an assistant for bathing, which was possible because of the Centre's equipment. My main job, however, was to go into homes of individuals who had been referred to the center and do an assessment of the level of care they needed.

Sitting in the pews of the White Rock Baptist church one Sunday,
I noticed after I got there that I didn't have a skirt on. Luckily, I
was wearing a long trench coat on. I had dressed in such a hurry,
putting on everything on for church attire, except a skirt.

1987

Later Frank decided to go into a furniture franchise called Price Busters. He really loved his store in Maple Ridge but sadly he put our house up again and this time we lost the house. The business was a great experience for Frank, but the franchisers didn't hold up their part of the bargain and we ended up with a lot of leftover furniture in our garage. We were able to sell some of it and what we did not sell we used to furnish our home.

The furniture franchise business worked for awhile. It was in maple Ridge it would have panned out if the main guy had not been so disorganized and so he shut the whole thing down. We had not planned at all for this stage of our lives, neither of us. I had always thought it was up to Frank to do this, but I was wrong.

I had nagged at him over the years to get an extra job or something on the side to add to our retirement. He did try a few times but only because of my prodding and pushing. He always attests, to this day, that whenever I asked him about doing something extra, he had said, "I am not a salesman, I cannot sell, I will not sell." Well, everything we do in life requires selling. Even in the health care field, you must sell yourself to the patient to build trust and confidence. Frank has such a friendly and easy-going personality that he can talk to almost anyone he meets. That is a kind of selling too.

So, we got involved in some pretty interesting business transactions and lost a lot of money in the process. It was just money we still have each other and that is the most important part.

We had moved to Walnut Grove to be closer to the Albion Ferry for Frank's commute, but after this all went down, the girls wanted to return to White Rock, so we bought a two-bedroom condo with an enclosed balcony. That was the best we could do. Jessica went to study music at Selkirk College in Nelson. She is an amazing singer and wasn't home very often and Karen was always planting trees in northern British Columbia.

After Evergreen Baptist and come share I moved onto my next business venture as a Christian bookstore owner. During the time that my family had had the party store, I had a section for Christian books and church supplies. It wasn't all that successful for many reasons, so when the main store closed, I moved across Johnston Road in White Rock to a little store that I called The Dove. I didn't have much collateral to do this sort of business but I thought I will try anyway.

A friend of my Dad's, very kindly lent me a nominal amount of money to help get it going, so I used it to stock the store with items that would bring people into the shop. To make a long story much shorter, the Dove flew the coup and I had to close. I was able to pay off the banks line of credit with returning all my product and selling off most of what was left, but I had to pay back Mr. Anonymous. The only way that I could see to do this was by calculating the value of the remaining stock and offer it to him. He was not overly happy with the arrangement, but he went for it in the end.

CHAPTER TWENTY-ONE

The Street Clinic

1992

I decided it was time to return to the field of nursing where I knew I could earn a regular income. I first worked at a long-term care facility in Fort Langley called Simpson Hospital. It was mostly nights, and, in fact, I think it was all nights and a lot of heavy work with the elderly who had mid-to-late dementia. I was saved by a phone call a few days into the job when I got a call from Colleen, a former colleague who was a bit of a rebel, to say the least. She had worked with me at Surrey Memorial years before, and she asked if I wanted to job-share at a needle exchange at the Surry Street Clinic in Surrey that also did HIV testing. Well, I thought about it, researched a bit, and said "Sure". She said I would just have to do an interview with her boss, Mr. Jim Bennett

I went for the interview at the Street Clinic. I was never quite sure how I landed this job, but I must have done well in the interview because they called me a few minutes after I got home and asked if I wanted to start on Monday. I was willing to do so.

I started completely on my own as Colleen did not work on Mondays. Then on Tuesday, I got a call from the boss saying, "Could you come in again today, Colleen has quit." Now I was the main person and a full-time nurse in a clinic where I had no idea what I was doing. Mr. Jim was an interesting man, an understatement for sure. I really got to like this man and we are still acquaintances to this day. Jim and I had our differences, but this work at the Street Clinic was probably my favorite job and right after that comes the time, I spent at Strathcona Mental Health.

When I first started working there, Mr. Jim was incredibly open about his way of running the office, but he wouldn't put up with any nonsense or something that he didn't think was right. If you crossed him, you were "toast "and out of there. There was a time when someone had donated a beautiful down quilt for one of the clients in the drop-in center. Well, there were three of us working that night, Karol, Darlene, and me, and one of us decided to exchange one of our own quilts for this beautiful one. Well, the third person decided to tell the boss and we were all reprimanded and had to return the quilt.

I did everything there. The clinic had been partly set up by Colleen, so I had a head start, but I did not have any training in doing the testing for Sexually Transmitted Diseases (STDs) on the street folk, so I was sent to the Vancouver General Hospital to be trained by the clinic experts there. What an eye opener! This was quite an experience; it was a two-week program that was hands-on and included a group of actors and actresses who were playing clients, so I got to do the mock tests on real individuals. This was a little weird though; everyone stood around and watched as one of us did the testing on an actor.

I was probably the first psychiatric nurse to have been through this program. I only say that because the physicians and the Boundary Health staff made a large fuss about me doing it because I was a psychiatric nurse, not a general nurse. The only real difference in the two training programs was the fact that we did not do the maternity portion of the curriculum. We did have one chapter or lesson on it, but that was it. Well, Gypsy Sue proved them wrong. Together, we had all the talent and skills of any other general duty nurse and after a while, they got over it.

When clients arrived at the Street Clinic, we had to do quite a long interview with each one who came to be tested for Human Immunodeficiency Virus (HIV) or Sexually Transmitted Disease (STD). Our clients included both males and females, lesbians, and gay men as well as transgenders and transsexuals. Even today, there is still a big scare with the AIDS virus, but it has "died" down a little. You don't hear the same panic as there was years ago but this may have to do with the fact that there are better drugs to help slow down the disease now, and people are getting educated earlier about prevention.

HIV prevalence rates vary dramatically across the world. The rate is more than 15 percent throughout southern Africa, compared with less than 2 percent in much of the rest of the world. Many of the people who came in who were female were choosing to have relationships with women, as they thought this would be safer way to prevent the spread of AIDS and HIV.

A particularly important part of the Street Clinic was the needle exchange and Karol Kuzyk an amazing little lady, had run it for about 20 years (1992-2012). Karol had a favorite saying, "What part of the exchange don't you understand?" She was a powerhouse of a personality to boot and had conquered many mountains in her life. She could handle the toughest clients. Karol and I went to Vancouver several times on the Skytrain for a few training sessions and on the trip home, we would look at each other and say, "Isn't that 10-29-1965 over there?". Then we would both smile and nod. We only knew the clients by their birthday dates and that kept everyone in the files anonymous. We were surprisingly good with this system. Mind you, we did know the names but they were not recorded.

Some of the clients were model users which is a bit of a contradiction since using an illegal substance was not a great way to stay healthy or lead a somewhat productive life. A few of the clients had 9 to 5 jobs and came into the needle exchange after work for more supplies and to drop off their used needles. These people, however, had so many issues that that did not enter into the equation of their life. Perhaps we have as many issues as they do but they have chosen to deal with them in ways that some of us would never even consider. It is a harsh life for sure.

There were a few favorite clients, those whose life choices we felt incredibly sad about. Clayton (not his real name) was much older than all the rest. In 1998, he would have been in his late 60's and so was playing with fire doing drugs and all the other tricks he did. He was a class act as well. He was an old Brit and his sister would come by periodically to see how he was and leave a few dollars for him. I never knew what had happened to him but I remember him clearly. He was truly lovely.

Then there was Marlene (not her real name). She was a young street worker. She had a couple of kids too. One time, twice now that I think of it, she came running in to me and said "Quick, quick, I need help." When I took her into the exam room and asked what was wrong, she said that she had put some cocaine in a pill box and put it into her vagina. Yes, that is what I said, her vagina. "Get it out of there quick," she said. So, I put her in the stirrups and got the speculum in place and worked around and finally found a little round yellow pill box and extracted it from her vagina. I automatically tossed it into the bin. "Don't do that," Marlene said. Oh my gosh, I grabbed it back and gave it to her. She was pleased with the results. She grabbed it and ran.

Another time she had done the same thing but not in a plastic pill container but with a surgical glove. We repeated the process and got the glove out but there was no cocaine. She was so mad and became quite accusatory about the cocaine, thinking that I tossed it. Then she realized it must have been absorbed into her vagina. She owed this cocaine to someone but too late this time.

A few years later I was working in a clinic in Langley and a young woman walked into the lobby of the clinic, looked at me, and said, "You don't recognize me?" I said, "Yes, I do. You are Marlene." I was just so shocked to see her and then it all came flooding back, my memory of her and all the times she came into the needle exchange for help. She had turned her life around, gone into a rehab treatment center, got some workplace training, and now was working in the area. She was seeing one of the psychiatrists for maintenance care. We chatted and had a lovely connection. The experience of the speculum was barely mentioned. I have never seen her since. I pray that she is alright, that this was another success case, that she was no longer on the streets, and that she is clean and sober. It is so wonderful to see the transition of these individuals who have had such a difficult journey.

Many of us in society who have had an easier journey can be very quick to point fingers, but no one knows another person's reality until they "walk a mile in someone else's shoes." Spending time trying to consider or understand another person's perspectives, experiences, or motivations is so important before judging them. I know that certain people can come across as selfish or mean-spirited but try walking a mile in their shoes before you dismiss them too quickly. No one chooses to be a drug addict.

I know of people who would not help another if their life depended on it, a sad characteristic to possess. Many of us feel we are superior to others. Sometimes that comes from always being put on a pedestal in our growing-up years or never being put in our place, whatever or wherever that may be. To look down on others is a flaw in their own character; they actually feel inferior themselves and must put others down to feel good.

Working at the street clinic really gave me an appreciation for life, people, and the fact that everyone has something to offer. People may have had a wonderful family life and they take a wrong turn onto the wrong path in life; then, there are those who never had a great start at all and have had to just figure it out on their own.

These are the people who are not always given the tools, or for that matter the rule book, that others have been provided with. It is good just to understand that we are all from a different cloth and to be reminded of that from time to time. We are all wired totally differently.

I really loved this job and enjoyed working with the clientele. One memory has stuck in my mind, actually there are many, but this one I won't forget. I was sitting in my office when a man in his later thirties, maybe even forty walked into the lobby and spoke to the receptionist, Bonnie, and asked to see me. I could hear the conversation as I was just around the corner. Bonnie asked me to come out and speak with him, I will call him John. He said he was told to come to this office, and I could help him with his marriage problems. I told him I was not really a marriage counsellor, but I would see what I could do. To this day I have no idea who sent him, maybe it was God himself. He was separated from his wife and children but wanted to go back to them but knew he needed to work on some issues first. At a point in the weekly sessions, John asked about my religious beliefs and wanted to know if I would pray with him and read from the bible too. Well, I never did tell my boss this because he was a little leery about my religious beliefs, but I did pray with Mike and read from the scriptures. He came on and off (scheduled) for about 8 months then he disappeared, and I did not hear from him for some time. He dropped by one day to thank me for my time and said he was back with his wife and children and he was working now. His was one of many success stories.

he came to the office and asked for me again. He brought me three red roses and said, "Thank you for what you have done for me." It was like something out of a novel. He then left, and I never saw him again.

The clinic eventually moved into to a new building across the street that was build specifically for the Street Clinic. It had a side yard and Jim sat in an office high above the clinic with a camera in his office that showed him what was going on in the back of the building most of the time. I remember one time that a client had over dosed on something, probably heroin in the day, and I was in my office. Suddenly I heard some screaming. I grabbed my mouthpiece and proceeded to perform CPR. I worked away on him and the timing was great. He woke up and looked me square in the face and said, "Why did you do that?" I said, "To save your life". By the time we had had this little interaction, the paramedics had arrived, and he was swooped up onto a stretcher and taken to Surrey Memorial Hospital. This was in mid-morning, and by 5 p.m. he was back again, ready for more. Having said all this, Jim came down to offer praises for my performance and said he had had a full view of everything that happened. My butt was in full view of the camera. It was a serious incident but the way I was positioned I had my derriere up in the air and Jim could see what was happening.

You wonder sometimes why we do the work we do but it is a necessary part of life and the job saves lives. This man came so close to dying, but the next day who should walk into the exchange for more clean paraphernalia but this man. It was eerie and it just boggled my mind at times.

One day while Karol, my co-worker, was chatting with a couple of male clients. They were talking quite loudly, so I jumped out of my chair and wandered into the exchange. The two men had about eight giant parcels of red meat. They had gone into the nearby Safeway grocery store and absconded with these and hoped that they would be able to sell them to us or anyone who could be persuaded to buy them. We, of course, would not and could not buy anything from these "salesmen". They left shortly after our conversation.

Another couple were, let us say famous at the clinic; I will call them Bonnie and Clyde. He was 6'6" and she was about 4'5" and they travelled together. They lived in the Buenavista Motel, which many years before was a decent second-rate motel but now was a flea bag place run by a sketchy older gentleman named Gunther. Clyde was very mistrusting of everyone. He had a long scar which ran from under his chin to the top of his skull. He told me that once when he was suicidal when he was high on some illegal substance, he took a rifle and stuck it up against his chin and let it blow. He was darn lucky to be alive. He was always doing something on the edge. Bonnie was just a tag-along as far as I could see. No family, no friends that could be trusted more than her, but we were kind and listened to them whenever they appeared at the door of the needle exchange.

One lovely young woman who was a regular heroin user and about 35 years old came in for clean needles. Once she came in asking for help. She shared that she had been diagnosed as bi-polar several years earlier but had refused to take the prescribed medications because they made her feel so helpless and they had side effects. Now, she said that she was starting to realize that the side effects from the heroin were not good for her and she wanted a better quality of life. So, I thought how can I help this lady. I suggested so go to Maple Ridge Treatment Center. Surprisingly enough, she went along with it. I got the application form and she went off. I heard from her several months later after she was clean and sober. She was grateful. There were a few success cases, but I discovered here that life is often all about Baby Steps. One step at a time. There are not many success cases from the street but this was one of them.

The Boundary Health Unit decided to restructure the clinics. The transition was not all that smooth, but the general nurses decided that psychiatric nurses were not able to give the hepatitis vaccine, so they would come in and do that. Sometime later, there was an uproar in the clinic when the staff in the drop-in center wanted a union, more money, and better benefits. I was the only nurse there so I became the only nurse who was part of the Hospital Employees Union (HEU).

It was during this upheaval that the Boundary Health nurses came into the clinic and took over running of it and they decided that the psychiatric nurse could not give the Hepatitis A and B injections. After a while, a backlog built up and vaccines were becoming outdated. The irony in this was when the union went to a tribunal with the Street Clinic, it was pointed out that I, as the street nurse on site, was administering Hep A and B vaccines. This came up in the court case, and I flatly denied using outdated vaccine since it was the Boundary Health nurses who administered all the vaccines. They were the ones who had used the out-dated vaccine.

The Hospital Employees Union seemed to be the best fit for this group of staff and I was the only nurse that was ever in the HEU so I guess I made history. When we were all dismissed, we took the Clinic to a hearing for compensation.

This was a very tough day. I was the one that was on the block for most of the hearing since I oversaw the clinic. One of the topics brought up was that "the hepatitis vaccines were outdated". I was not aware of this news and so was left with my tail between my legs on that one. I did not really know what to say, so I just said nothing. I was no longer in charge of administering the vaccine, but the issue of the vaccine being outdated was pointed out. I once again needed to speak up for myself but now I had learned a great deal in life, if not for me then for others. I maintained my composure and answered the questions and told the truth. Accusations were flying on that day in the tribunal. I had to sit at the round table with all the officials, Mr. Jim opposite me, and say how my words were the whole truth and nothing but the truth, so help me God?

The court hearing turned out well for me and the workers. I thought it was good. I got a month's salary, so I took my mom to Thailand to visit with our daughter and her granddaughter, Jessica, who was on vacation from a school in Taiwan. The others did get a settlement as well. We never discussed the settlement with each other.

The night after the hearing I was at home and the phone rang. It was Mr. Jim wanting to apologize for having me put through all that drama. He went on to reminisce about all the good times at the clinic and what a great job we had done, and on and on, and how he was going to go into the ministry. He was so nice and pleasant, and although we had such a great conversation, I was very guarded, honest but protective. I was also a little miffed that he had not been more supportive of me in this case, but it was what it was. He said he was going to eventually leave the clinic and return to study at Trinity.

Well, he did do that. He became an ordained minister of the Anglican Church of Canada. People do change. When I first started working at the Street Clinic, he had a jaded approach to religion. When I left the clinic, Jim went back to Trinity Western University and studied religion. He used to ask me regularly if God was with me. He later hired a former friend of mine who also was a Christian and went to the same church. Strange though, when I lost my job at the needle exchange, she suddenly decided that we did not know each other. People change. She and her family had spent an entire weekend at our cabin in Washington State. I guess we all must pick our battles.

It was sad when my job at the clinic came to an end abruptly after five years, but things always happened for a reason. I had to leave the Street Clinic, which was unfortunate, since I really enjoyed this job, but the government was making new guidelines and wanted the public health nurses to operate the clinic. This clinic went from employing one nurse, me, to about four nurses, doing the job I did.

We are never sure what the reason is. There are no mistakes in life; everything happens just as it is supposed to happen. This is my belief, and I am sticking to it.

Here is another anecdote that I must share. I did not know about it until a few years later when I am working in Langley Mental Health. One day when I was coming to work, I saw a young woman, Marcy (not real name) in the waiting room and I did a double-take and said hello. Marcy offered information on how she was doing. She said she was clean and sober and had been for several years now. She added that she had gotten married and continued to do well. She looked great. Success stories like this in my line of work are great to see and there are lots more of them. The negative stories, however, are usually the ones that people focus on and they are impressed by the sensationalism of the details.

I always felt safe when walking to my car. The clients trusted us and so they were not going to ruin the bond we had together.

My former boss, Mr. Jim, was such funny guy (meaning great sense of humor) and we had so many great laughs together. I was privileged to work with and for him in the community. I was really pleased when I learned that he had been given "The 2020 Good Citizen Award. Jim Bennett has volunteered for over 30 years and has served on numerous committees, boards, and community projects. He has also founded two major community organizations and raised hundreds of thousands of dollars to support the most vulnerable citizens living in the City of Surrey. Over the years, Mr. Bennett has received many awards, including the Queen Elizabeth II Golden Jubilee Medal, and is still serving the community today as the Trust Administrator for the Jim Bennett Trust Fund."

CHAPTER TWENTY-TWO

Back to the Hospital

After leaving the Street Clinic, I went back to work at Surrey Memorial Hospital (SMH). I initially worked on the Inpatient Unit only on a casual basis, waiting ever so patiently for a permanent position. It was not easy to wait as I am an impatient person especially when it comes to wanting a job. Finally, the opportunity came to work in the Psychiatric Emergency Department which was right up my alley. I loved it there except there was a lot of shift work and I wanted to work only day shift. As a result, I started to do some casual shifts at the Mental Health office where it was only Monday to Friday, just like bankers. That is the way it used to be, but now they also work weekends and some evenings. Poor them.

I had some great experiences in the Emergency Department too. One that sticks in my mind is a girl named Rosanne who was well known in Emergency and in the Inpatient Unit. One night, she arrived in a police cruiser in hand cuffs and not in the usual fashion either. She was in the back of the cruiser, hog tied with both her hands and feet cuffed behind her. To get her into the Emergency Department, it was necessary to put her on a stretcher for transport. It was quite the sight to see this young girl, hand and feet behind her, rocking to and fro on the stretcher. When she reached the hallway for check in, all we heard were expletives, "F… Y..! F… Y..!" and her words to the police officers, "Don't touch me, you filthy pigs!" She was always a bit of a drama queen and wanted an audience. Well, she got one that night. The staff did not take off the cuffs until she calmed down and was safely settled in the Security Room.

I loved this part of working in the Emergency at SMH. There was never a dull moment and always something new every day. Well, except for the clients who were repeat… repeat… repeat. And that is to be expected. They are in a cycle. When they feel well, they take their meds; they are in a "honeymoon phase" and feeling good, so good and they say to themselves, "I don't need this medication!" Then they stop their meds and before they know it, they are sliding down hill again. It is a slippery slope.

Another day, I was the only psychiatric nurse on and the general nurses were a little snobbish about these patients, maybe even afraid of them. One boy, who I will call a boy although he was about 22, was psychotic and came to the Emergency accompanied by the RCMP. He was higher than a kite, a bad expression, and was put into the seclusion room for his own safety and the safety of others. He had been taking meds but like so many others, decided he did not need them and had started to take methamphetamines instead. When I arrived in the early morning hours, the head nurse said she needed my help. I looked on the screen and saw this 6-foot 4-inch buff young man, naked and totally covered in feces, yes feces, … and she wanted me to go in and clean him up. Oh, this is what I got the big bucks for. Mmmmmm … yes, I understand now. So, with the help of the security boys, who were immensely helpful, we escorted him to a shower room. I had a rubber apron on. He was quite co-operative for the task at hand. The security guards were smirking to themselves. Inside, I was smirking too, but I could not let it out until I was all done cleaning him up.

On another occasion, I was at the Nurses' Station and curtains surrounded the stall in front of the desk. All I could hear was a buzzing noise …. wir, wir, wir. I said to one of the other staff nurses,

"What is that noise?" No one said anything out loud, but they pointed to the file indicating I should read the chart. It reported that the man, in his mid 40's, had put a ridiculously small vibrator up his anus and it was in the "on" position. He could not get it out. Here he was, needing to have it surgically removed. How embarrassing this was for him. There was a lot of smirking and tittering in Emergency that morning. Apparently, it is quite the thing for men, and maybe women, to put a motor in their anus and it gives them sexual pleasure. Well, not this "chickee". I am too straight for that. It was crazy making. We had to listen to the "wir, wir, wir" from behind the curtains until it was time for him to go up for surgery.

On a sad note, I was asked to go into an exam room and stay with a Dad whose baby daughter had passed away. She was all swaddled and lying on the exam table. He was broken right there and he was probably in shock. I never knew where the mother was and I didn't ask either. I was in shock myself. I had seen dead bodies before but not babies. This was a first. I will never forget the vision.

During all this time, I was only working part time, 4 out of 5 days, instead of a full-time and so the other days I would venture into Vancouver and look after my Aunt Grace who was slipping rapidly into dementia. She still lived in her own house and loved to go shopping. On a moment's whim, she would call and say, "Can you take me to The Bay?" She loved to look at the jewellery and all the bling. She would purchase something every time and on one occasion, we saw these silver coffee table dishes. She had to have one and thought I should too and offered to buy it for me. They were very pretty and so I said, "Oh sure, get me one, Auntie Grace." I still have it somewhere. Another time she called because I had forgotten that I was supposed to meet up with her. Immediately I jumped into my car and headed into Vancouver in my little 1995 Cavalier in the HOV lane. Suddenly, I had a light bulb go off and realized I was driving in the fast lane and there was only one person in my car, ME. Quickly without causing any harmful damage to anyone I moved over into the regular lane. I made the trip to Auntie Grace's place in record time.

She was a gem, my Auntie Grace. I was the one she always recognized when we would go out for supper with the family. Sometimes when my sister-in-law would come to visit with her, she would say, "Oh, I remember you. You are Elaine. How are you doing?" Well, it turns out that Elaine was a school chum from when she was growing up in Halifax. You may ask yourself, "Now, why are you telling us about Auntie Grace?" Well, her dementia became much more severe, and it was not safe to leave her alone in her own home. She would call 911 on a whim and say that her husband was alone in the house across the street, or when she was afraid, she would call 911. I knew a few people who worked the 911 desk, and they were receiving so many calls from her that they contacted me. We got the ball rolling and found someone to come and assess Auntie Grace for a place in a nursing home where she could get care. She really needed some help. We did manage to find someone who would come and take her out once a week. Her name was Remy, and she was a real blessing to us. She worked at the STAT center for the respite care of the people with dementia so she was familiar with dementia and had the training to take Auntie Grace out once a week for an outing.

The doctors and psychiatrist assessed her after a short interval, and we continued to keep a watchful eye on her. We did go out for supper every weekend to Hy's Steak House. The staff there were aware of her status as well. Sometimes we took her to Vancouver Community College fine dining, and our dear friend, Peter, who worked there as an instructor would wait on us, or at least monitor the students in-training.

One Friday night, we took it upon ourselves to take some clothes and essentials into Vancouver for her. We planned to stay with her this one night in the one-bedroom suite in her basement. It was an interesting house. Her husband had built the basement first, (well of course), but they had lived in the basement until the main floor was completed. She was not, however, going to have any part of us staying there, so we went back home. She was very private, enormously proud, and didn't really understand why we needed to be there.

The following week she was given a spot at the Vancouver General STAT Center day care where she would go daily. This would have been all well and good, but the same day that she was to start there, we got a phone call saying that she had a place at Broadway Manor, a genuinely nice care facility on Nanaimo and Broadway. It was really a lovely place. When she left the STAT center, she thought she was going home. Remy did the transporting and stayed with her until we arrived. She was a little confused in the beginning but it went well. Initially. she had a double room but the very next day she got her own private room.

The transition went very well. She did not seem to notice anything out of the ordinary, but she did notice that it was not her own place. We had taken some things from her house that would be familiar to her the night she moved there: a lamp, a chair, and a few ornaments. I went to see her pretty much every day after work and she was always very happy to see me.

I decided to change workplaces so we could be closer to Auntie Grace. So rather than leave her house empty, Frank and I moved into it with Frankie, the little dog we got from Taiwan. I needed to work close to her so I got a lead on a position in Vancouver through a friend of a friend and was asked to come in for an interview. It was a gruelling interview at Strathcona Mental Health team on Heatley Street. I had not ever had an interview like it before except when I was interviewing for the Vancouver Housing Society where I had to go before a Board and present an essay entitled, "Not in My Backyard".

Back to the Strathcona interview. There were 7 people around the table and I was placed at the head of the table. There were three doctors, a couple of nurses, the Director, and the Deputy Director of the clinic. I had to answer many skill testing questions and then had to teach them about the Mental Health Act.

*What is the **Mental Health Act**? The Mental Health Act is the law that describes what should happen when someone who is living with a mental illness needs treatment and protection for themselves/others. In Canada, every province has a mental health law that is used to serve the people living in that province.*

I was given an easel and a felt pen and told to teach them. I had to stand up in front of all these people and teach them about the Mental Status Exam and all the details of it. At the risk of being boastful, I have to say I did a darn good job. One thing I had learned over the years about job interviews was to say too much, or at least ramble on, because the more you said, the more points you would get.

When I got home from the interview, only about 10 minutes by car away, I received a phone call from Ralph Buckley, the director, "Would you like the job as case manager?" Of course, I said yes. This was my other stellar job.

Right away, I just up and left the Surrey Mental Health Team. I was not doing a permanent job there, just a casual one, and the manager said, "Give it a try and if you don't like it, well, you can always try to get back." It was such a "cool" place to work right downtown in the east side of Vancouver where the harshest of the harshest live and stroll the streets where everyone knew everyone, and they not only protected themselves but knew everyone's business to protect their own back. The Salvation Army, the Union Gospel Church, the United Church, the Anglican church, and the Catholic Churches were all doing their part to save these souls and to feed them too. Some churches would not let their clients have any free food unless they first listened to a God message first. I have mixed feeling about his. Mother Theresa wouldn't have done that. She would have accepted them right where they were in the moment.Is that not a form of mindfulness?

__Mindfulness__ is a type of __meditation__ in which you focus on being intensely aware of what you are sensing and feeling in the moment, without interpretation or judgment. __Practicing mindfulness__ involves breathing methods, guided imagery, and other __practices__ to relax the body and mind and help reduce stress. The oldest documented evidence of the practice of meditation are found in the wall arts in the Indian subcontinent from approximately __5,000__ to __3,500__ BCE, which show people seated in meditative postures with half-closed eyes. Written evidence of any form of meditation is first seen in the Vedas around __1500 BCE__. advocating putting forth a hand of kindest and always being there in their time of need and neglect.

Part of my introduction to the job included walking the streets with the staff to find out what the lay of the land was and so I was introduced to many weird and wonderful sights of life. It just kept getting better. Our walk was along Hastings Street and into some of the less desirable restaurants for people in my circle but that is how it goes. I would have stayed on until retirement, but Auntie Grace's house, the one we were living in, sold so we had to find another place to live. Our solution was to move back to Langley where we found ourselves a sweet little rancher in our price range. We did not have much of a down payment but at this time in the real estate market we were able to purchase a house without a down payment, a pretty dangerous thing to do financially. Our mortgage payments would, however, be too high for us to keep paying once we retired so that was something to keep in mind

My new job was on the Strathcona Mental Health team, my other most favourite job, next to the street clinic. It was a great location because my work place was only about a 5-minute drive and Broadway Manor was nearby too. I could have walked to work, but I needed the car to visit clients. This was such a wonderful job I loved going to work everyday.

A documentary about the Downtown East Side called the "Through the Blue Lens" explores the area was and is, a culture unto itself, a true community down there. The film documents a year of life and death on the streets and behind tenement walls.

A striking aspect of the film is not only the horror of drug abuse but the story of how the interaction between the police and the people who are living with complex substance abuse and mental health diagnoses and how the camera acted as a catalyst and actually changed the people involved. The cops became more sympathetic to the people on the street and their complex barriers to care. When friendship was extended to them by the police and film makers, they developed self-esteem and, in some cases, were able to move towards recovery. This documentary was made during the height of the then unpublished scandal of the missing women in downtown Vancouver.

Grant you, the situation working the Downtown East side of Vancouver is a little different than Mother Theresa's working the streets of Calcutta; however, I still feel that it is better to feed the stomachs first and then the souls. Attacking the stomachs of the poor and downtrodden souls is a kind of emotional warfare. I have somewhat the same philosophy as Mother Theresa. "They will come when they are ready."

This always made me think of how the Catholic Church and other churches went into villages of the First Nations people in northern Canada and pretty much kidnapped the children, taking them to residential schools. I am not sure what they told them about religion but the church schools seemed to think they knew how to raise the Aboriginal children better than the parents themselves.

Residential schools *were established with the assumption that Aboriginal culture was unable to adapt to a rapidly modernizing society. It was believed that their children could be successful if they assimilated into mainstream Canadian society by adopting Christianity and speaking English or French. So, in much the same way, making the poor people of the street listen to a message before they can eat is* blackmail.

The staff at Strathcona, downtown on the east side of Vancouver, were remarkably diverse and we were a Team in the true meaning of the word. We worked as a team, right from the top down to the newest newbies. Even the doctors were right in there helping with team work and spirit. This is the one thing that comes to my mind when I think of my time there.

I was still working at Strathcona when I started to train for the half marathon (that was in 2006), sponsored by the Leukemia and Lymphoma Society. I had seen it advertised in the newspaper and thought I would check it out. I would have to raise at least $5000 dollars as well as the cost of my flight and hotels in Phoenix, Arizona. This was something out of my safety zone. I was not a marathon runner, but I did have the option walk or run but I chose to run. It was a chance to do something for a great cause ... and get into better physical condition. I had to train regularly, and it meant a lot of commitment on my part. I had to travel to Vancouver once a week to meet with the team and we all trained together. On my own I had to go through some paces to follow a training schedule. I also had to raise 5000 dollars. I did this by sending out fund raising letters to as many friends and family I felt would support my cause. I was quite thrilled with the response. I also planned, with the help of many friends, a pub night at the Fort Langley Pub. I raised the amount and 1600 dollars more by the time I had to leave for the marathon. The other exciting factor was that the race was on my birthday, January 15. The run was called the Rock and Roll run and all along the route there were bands playing music. It truly was a fun experience. So glad I did it. My time wasn't all the wonderful 2 hours and a half but I finished I t and that was the point.

I recall one time that a group from the Emanuel Church in White Rock, a group I was part of, went to the Union Gospel Mission one afternoon to serve dinner to the street people. A great long line of people wound all the way around the building and down Powell Street. When it was time, people were let into the building, but they had to go into the chapel first before they could have any food. It was our dear departed Pastor, Albert Josephson, who was preaching that night, and he was an extraordinarily strong Christian.

Throughout the service while he was preaching, a few back benchers heckled Albert. Some of them were asked to leave but others settled down and waited until it was time. Then they were ushered into the dining room. There were many of us serving up the food and some of the clients wanted seconds to take home. We provided them with paper plates so they could take home the extra meal.

CHAPTER TWENTY-THREE

Strathcona Days

One day, when we were looking for one of our clients, my work buddy went to the residence where he lived, and of course, he was not there, but the strangest thing happened. Two Vancouver Police officers came to the door and asked for me and then asked if I would step outside for a few minutes. "Sure," I said, and we went out on the back stoop and chatted for a few minutes. Well, this was a time when my shoulders changed posture so rapidly. I can still recall how they moved forward. What the officers told me was that the client I was looking for had been found dead under some rose bushes that morning only a few blocks from the house. He had been there for several days and it looked like an overdose of cocaine. He had been very depressed, and he had always felt he had let his family down, first by being depressed which was a slur on the culture to admit this, and secondly by the fact that he had not made anything of himself to this point in his life. He had served in the Canadian Navy for a brief time, but had been discharged and, if I remember correctly, it was not an honourable discharge. He was chronically depressed and Dr. Kirkpatrick, with whom we worked, was always trying to encourage him to stay on his meds and change his focus so he could perhaps take up an occupation. He was a heavy smoker too, so this did not help with his sleep pattern. The entire team knew this client well and were not surprised that he had died, but still there had to be an investigation when a client suicided while under the care of the team.

The one thing I remember about Dr. Kirkpatrick is that whenever a client came into our office, Dr. K would always ask them, "Do you have any dreams?" I always remember that and have used that often in my own practice too.

One thing we all need to keep on the top burner is our dreams so we can forge ahead. There are many benefits that come from dream experiences, and the most beneficial, in my opinion, is the opportunity to play out a variety of choices and scenarios in an "arena" where our resistance is minimal. For example, a dream of being able to fly can give us the feeling of freedom, empowerment, a perspective of reality, a realization of the availability of choices, and perhaps, how easy a choice can be. We may wake up and take that feeling to work and then be inspired to be super creative, be successful at new and having fun doing it. This is how we can use our dream experiences to excel in our waking reality. Same goes for a nightmare; we can use the information to empower ourselves. Again, it is a perfectly fine choice to not engage with our dreams; personally, I cannot imagine living my life without them.

This client's story was featured on the show Divinci's Inquest on CBC, but it was totally anonymous to protect the privacy of the client and the family.

Some clients are more imprinted than others in our minds.

A female client was a diabetic and bi-polar. She was sweet and a client of Tom Waterson. Generally, she was quite reliable with her medications. She had little family or friends, and she relied heavily on the help from the Strathcona Team. We connected well and she depended on me for a lot. She did have a son who was involved from a distance.

After I left the clinic, I went to work in the Emergency Department of the Memorial Hospital in Surrey. The position was as a triage nurse for psychiatric patients. I did love this job as well. I know I had my favorite jobs but I loved all my jobs, loved the people. It was so riveting and challenging to go to work everyday. There were no two days the same. I had a great way with the patients, but I did have to ask for the help of the security boys (they were great support) on many occasions and the RCMP as well.

The last place I worked before my retiring from full time work was Langley Mental Health and I will say it now since I am officially retired. The staff I worked with were great, especially my immediate superior, Kathy, and the members on the Adult Team, but the management itself was dreadful. She was so unapproachable, did not appreciate any laughter, or support socialization among the staff., Now that did not bode well with Miss Social Butterfly, that would be me. I started a great pre-work coffee group which lasted only until the manager thought she needed to micromanage. It did not matter that we were taking good care of the clientele. It was more important to run a tidy and clean ship and forget about the welfare of the clients. This is what was missing in the mental health. It was more important to have a great management assessment than to see what the client wanted or needed. There were always changes being made but none of these "changers", as I will call them, had any idea what was happening on the frontlines. I stayed there three years and then retired from full time work. I retired early; sometimes I regret this since my pension is tiny but what is money.

It was then my husband and I moved to the East Coast of Canada. We had had a few financial setbacks, so we were not able to own an affordable house in the Langley area on our little pensions. So, we decided a year before retiring that we would search for a home in New Brunswick that we could afford on our pensions. We found the home of our dreams and now live here. It is a little log house on 4 acres, a little piece of paradise. My parents did not want us to leave the West Coast, nor did my bestie, Sandy. She was stoked. I sometimes think "Why did we do it?", but it was a good financial move. Emotionally it was tough but leaving all my wonderful friends behind was so hard. I have made some new great friends here, but the old ones are solid in my heart of hearts. Especially my movie star groupies. I have certainly had many life experiences and hope to continue with more.

When we first moved to the East Coast, it was all very new, and we had lots to do. Well, unpacking was number one on the agenda.

CHAPTER TWENTY-FOUR

Auntie Grace

One thing we all need to keep on the top burner is our dreams so we can forge ahead. There are many benefits that come from dream experiences, and the most beneficial, in my opinion, is the opportunity to play out a variety of choices and scenarios in an "arena" where our resistance is minimal. For example, a dream of being able to fly can give us the feeling of freedom, empowerment, a perspective of reality, a realization of the availability of choices, and perhaps, how easy a choice can be. We may wake up and take that feeling to work and then be inspired to be super creative, be successful at new and having fun doing it. This is how we can use our dream experiences to excel in our waking reality. Same goes for a nightmare; we can use the information to empower ourselves. Again, it is a perfectly fine choice to not engage with our dreams; personally, I cannot imagine living my life without them.

I kept an eye on Aunt Gracie's finances and personal life, but also, they were closely monitored by a public trustee. During this time while we lived there, we were under the scrutiny of the public trustee, so we had to be careful about all our spending. I sure was careful and submitted all the necessary paperwork. Someone once said to me, "Sure is nice being able to live there rent free." Well, I never felt it was rent free. I had her finances to see to, the paperwork to complete, and I looked after her. Some days, I would take her shopping but I mostly did the shopping she asked for, brought to her room for her to try on, and then returned what didn't fit. I did personal shopping for her as well. Every night, I went to the nursing home to visit and sometimes I stayed for supper. I also attended all the community planning meeting at the nursing home and looked after her home as well. Oh, I mean I did not live rent free, so I replied, "Well, if you want to live here and look after Aunt Grace you can?" Well, that changed the conversation very quickly.

When we lived in the house that had been Aunt Gracie's, you will never guess what we found? we found the ashes from Uncle Ludwick and cousin Christine in the cupboard of the fake fireplace. They had been there for years.

But having said all that, shortly after this conversation, we got served with papers from the Public Trustee for misuse of funds. That opened a can of worms, literally. We ended up going to court over several months and we had to hire two different lawyers, and they both took us down different paths of recovery …. and to the cleaners. Frank paid a big price as he went through this whole ordeal, and my parents endured a lot of stress. I had to submit financials for the entire time we had been looking after Aunt Grace. I put on about 30 pounds and started to become quite distant in my relationship with my husband.

Auntie Grace passed away in March. We got a phone call from the nursing home one Sunday morning as we were all leaving for church, and the nurse said, "I am sorry to say Mrs. Zdebiak passed away this morning". Frank and I headed over to Mom and Dad's townhouse and then got in a caravan headed for Broadway Manor where Grace had been living. We all went up to the third floor and found her in her room covered with a bedspread. She had got up, dressed herself, fallen to the floor, and had a heart attack She had gone peacefully.

Court Case.

This was a disaster. We had moved into Aunt Grace's house to help her and look after her house. We renovated it and that increased the value of her estate. We looked after her, took her shopping, and visited her everyday. She had no family, no one. We were all she had. Someone, however, had called the trustee, Doris Wong, and said we were taking money from the estate. We took nothing. All the money that was spent on the nursing home and looking after her. We are still unsure who would do such a thing. It ended up in a court case, saying we had to pay back rent to Grace. This was all very upsetting to us.

I think it was around this time that Frank started to lose his hearing. He did not respond much of my conversation and I almost felt ignored by him. We finally got this all settled, and then we were reprimanded for "not paying rent". I had never even given it a thought. After all, we were looking after my Auntie and also fixing up her house, so it was safe and liveable again. This was a case of darned for what you do and darned for what you do not do.

Frank was working for Forensic Hospital Services during this period after we moved from the Vancouver house to the house we bought in Langley. He worked there about 16 years before retiring. During that time, he would never take or change his days off to weekends. So, in 16 years, we never had a weekend off together. I did not think that was too much to as but he would never rock anyone's boat. He was in a schedule and would not ask to make any concessions to have same time off as me.

This is one of my rants as you can see. I was working full time at Langley Mental Health after leaving Strathcona Mental Health while I was living in Vancouver. After the blessed court case finished, we sold the house and moved back to Langley. I loved both jobs but only changed because it was nearer our home in Langley. During that time, I did extra work when needed at Langley but it was not nearly as busy or as time-consuming as the Strathcona job. So, "Idle hands are the work of the devil".

Idle hands are the devils' workshop, idle lips are his mouthpiece. Regardless of its source it means that one who is idle will likely come to do evil.

*This **proverb** is thought by some to come from the Bible, the book of Proverbs, Chapter 16 Verse 27; however, this is probably a misreading, driven by an application of Protestant theological assumptions. Only in the 1971 Living Bible was the idea injected into its translation.*

CHAPTER TWENTY-FIVE

A Few Extra
Chronological Notes

1990

I was getting nervous now so thought that instead of leaving any of the inheritance where it would be accessible to someone else, I thought we, as a family, would benefit from a recreation property. We had rented one in the State of Washington a few times previously and quite liked the area near Mount Baker. This is where we looked and eventually, we bought our ski and summer lodge. We bought at the right time when the US dollar was down, but 15 years later it was a different story. We lost a lot of money when we sold the cabin, but we must remember that we had 15 great years there. The kids loved that place. Many guests stayed over with us, and the kids had their friends stay over as well. When Jessica had completed her year at Bible College, she invited, the entire class to the cabin or it seemed like it to me. The next time that we drove up ourselves to enjoy the place, we could detect this horrendous odor from the road. It was the hot tub. There had been at least 10-12 in it at any one time over a five-day period and no one had put any chemicals in it the entire time. We had to drain the tub, clean it, and refill it.

So now we are insanely cautious if we get involved in any business deals Too many have led us down the garden path to bankruptcy. Frank is such a kind person, trusting all the wrong people, and believing that if someone said it then it must be true. Well, I am a little more skeptical. I guess it comes from working in the field of assessment all my life. It makes for remarkably interesting conversations at times with lots of people from all walks of life. But then I have become a little more jaded than the average person. Having said that, Frank is a little package of anxiety, not really that little either he is 6 foot 4 inches, maybe only 6 foot 3 inches and a half now that he is almost 3 score and 10 years old now. Is that what you call long in the tooth. We are all getting that way as time goes by, the Lord willing.

2007

The year was 2007 and I was working full-time at the mental health clinic in Langley, BC. My dear husband was working at the forensic hospital so we both had stressful jobs. He worked shift work so we didn't have a lot of time off together nor were our holidays always together. That made for a lot of free time for me and made it possible to spend time with my crazy girlfriends. Our own girls were gone from home and grown up, so our time to retire was starting to look at us down the barrel of a Winchester rifle fully loaded.

We really had not planned our retirement and we were poor money organizers. Plus, I had cashed in my pension earlier in my career since Frank had hit a rough patch and we needed some cash. This was such a bad choice. Life has consequences and with our choices, that meant that I now have an exceedingly small monthly pension. I was still ready to retire and maybe work later. My mom always said work until you are 70. Now that is the story in a nutshell so stay tuned for the rest of the tale as it unfolds before your eyes.

I loved my job. It had been my passion for almost 30 years, and it had gotten to the point where the management at the health care team really did not have the same passion for the clients. It was all about the smooth running of the office: micro-managing the staff, peaking through cracks in the doorways, listening beside the offices or outside the staff kitchen at lunch time. It was always "Be careful. "She's listening", "shut the door. She may hear you." She did not even wish me well or tell me I did a great job on the Team when I retired. I know that I did in fact do a good job because the clients still remember me with great fondness and my successor was so impressed because I had done a case review on every client before she took over my client list. I think that is confirmation enough. It was no fun working under these conditions.

Frank and I had a dream to retire to the east coast of Canada. Sounds like Martin Luther King "I had a dream", but a little different when I sang it. I love the East Coast. It is quiet, peaceful and no hustle and bustle.

"I Have a Dream" is a public speech that was delivered by American civil rights activist Martin Luther King Jr. during the March on Washington for Jobs and Freedom on August 28, 1963, in which he called for civil and economic rights and an end to racism in the United States.

The summer of 2008 our extended family, the Pyche branch, had a family reunion. This is one time my dear wonderful grandmother would have loved to have been there to see all the grandkids, nieces, and nephews. She had a lot to do with the growing up and caring for the girls in the Pyche family in Prince Albert, Saskatchewan. She kept a record of all the Pyche births. marriages, and other special events, especially about Catherine, the oldest of Ralph's children. There were, in fact, four other daughters and one of them, Marion, was quite sickly, as the story goes. One winter, Grandma said she could stay with Marion in town. She stayed for some time and then when her father came to town one day, Marion was peering out the window and yelled with somewhat a gleeful tone "It's uncle Ralph!" Well, that was the end of Marion's staying in town. Uncle Ralph whisked her up and took her home.

The reunion was in August 2008 and the "cousins" in Peterborough did such a wonderful job of arranging everything. Mom, Dad, Frank and I travelled together. My brother couldn't get the time off to come and as far as we knew neither did his wife. Too bad it would have been great to have our entire family.

I had planned to continue to New Brunswick after the get-together to look for a house for our retirement. Frank did not want to make the trip, so he did not ask for the time off. After the reunion, the four of us went to Ottawa to visit our daughter's in-laws and stayed the night there. We had a lovely visit with Bernie and Leona. It was very generous of them to open their home to us. In the morning, we drove Frank to the airport so he could fly home and go back to work. The three of us then continued our journey to visit the Maritimes.

2009

After our trip to Moncton in July 2009, Frank and I returned home with great excitement since we had purchased our new forever home in Boundary Creek, NB. It was a log home on 4 acres of forested land. It was beautiful spot, and all our precious stuff was in storage, so we thought that rather than pay storage any longer, we would take the stuff to the East Coast in the fall. We planned to fly, and we were booked for October. We headed for the East Coast. The moving truck we ordered was supposed to arrive the same time as we did. Well, that was not the case. We were there almost 10 days before the truck arrived.

We did many other things while we were there. We got ourselves new beds for both bedrooms. Alta, our wonderful angel who lived in Riverview, loaned us some furniture: a picnic table and chairs. I had my laptop so we could watch movies. Most evenings and overnight, we stayed at Alta and Charlie's place but once we got the beds we stayed at the new house. It was just like camping. We did not have much, but it was fun puttering about the property and waiting patiently for the furniture to arrive. We were not sure about who would stay in the house after we were back in Langley for the year, so we put an ad in the paper and got a few responses. We chose a couple who brought a resumé with them and said they both had jobs. We were rather desperate to find tenants as the days were flying by and we were scheduled to return home soon. We really took a chance when we left this couple that we had only met for about 25 minutes to look after our house. We had our entire livelihood in the house, everything we owned. I know it was just things, but they were our things. So, we stepped out of the box and let them stay. It was a bit risky and naïve. We did not even know these people, only met them at the door once and agreed. They did not do any damage to the property. This was a bonus, and all our possessions were intact so we had a lot to be thankful about.

Finally, on the Thursday just prior to leaving, our furniture arrived, and everything was piled into the garage or put into the house for storage. Hindsight says that we should have just left everything in boxes, and we could have unpacked the following year when we returned after retirement. Things always have a way of working out.

We returned home to our jobs and continued to stay at Sandy's place. We were renting two of her rooms, one was for our clothes and office stuff and the other was the bedroom. It was great staying there We even had our little dog Frankie with us.

I felt maybe it would be good to move in with my mom and Dad until we left for the East again in May of 2010. It would give us more time to spend with my parents so that was the plan.

We continued to work at our jobs and made further plans to discontinue all things that needed to be done. We both retired on the same day with parties in our respective offices. Frank was quite surprised by his. I had an inkling of what was transpiring at mine. I was given a few lovely gifts from the office staff and one of the doctors who was on the geriatric team very generously gave me some gas gift cards and Walmart gift cards. We were driving across the country, after all, so these were perfect gifts. A week before completing our jobs our good friends gave us a lovely going away party at Andrea and Mike's home. My parents also were in attendance too. Many of my friends knew my parents and some of them played bridge with them so everyone knew each other. It was great to have such a lovely relationship with my parents that they would socialize with us many places.

Years later, a dear friend named Yvonne always liked to call me Gypsy Sue, I am not sure why except for the fact that I have moved around a lot in my career since its inception over the last 35 years. I always was with the same health authority except for a three-year term when I lived in Vancouver and worked for the Vancouver Coastal Health Authority. This was only because I felt the call to move into my Aunt's house and care for her home and her while she had early to mid onset of dementia.

After this I returned to the Fraser Health Authority. OH yes, there was another time when there were not any full-time positions at Surrey Memorial, so I worked for a non- profit clinic. This job at the Street Clinic was probably my favorite job of all but it was challenging to say the least.

We moved a lot. I think I counted 23 times in our more 40 odd years of marriage and during those moves we did have a couple of long stays, and by long, I mean 3 or 4 years. The longest stay was in White Rock, B.C. where we stayed for 8 years. It was my most favorite place ever. Our last move to the east coast was supposed to be our last move and moving home address.

Prior to our trip to the East Coast, I had been in touch with a realtor named Rob Anderson. He showed me many places in the Moncton area. Some were beachfront near Shediac. My favourite one was close to the beach, but Frank was very into the research that was done by Al Gore, former US Vice President, who said that sea levels were going to rise and take over the land. Gore had produced a documentary called the Inconvenient Truth.

An Inconvenient Truth *is a 2006 American documentary film directed by Davis Guggenheim about the former United States Vice President Al Gore's campaign to educate people about global warming. The film features a slide show that. Al Gore has presented over 1,000 times to audiences worldwide Some inland properties would actually become waterfront properties. That was not too good. We settled for something in the country and within driving distance of the beach. I wasn't too successful in finding a place, but I did get a good look at the area so that when we were home we would know where the places we saw on the Internet were.*

Later in October of the same year, Frank took a trip on his own and checked out houses as well. He was not successful either but now we had an overall picture. Se we decided to go down together in the spring of 2009 and buy a house. We looked at quite a few and even looked in Memramcook and Dorchester where the maximum-security penitentiary is located. We looked in Shediac where I had hoped to buy originally but I still felt that it was too close to the coast and would be affected by global warming and coastal flooding of the properties. Finally, we settled on a place called Boundary Creek. It had always been Frank's dream to live in a log house, so when we found this one, we decided to buy it. It had four acres of land and a large double garage with a workshop in the back. He would be all set. We made an offer, but the seller wanted one thousand dollars more than our offer. Of course, we took it. It may have been what made her break even, so we gave it to her anyway. She had a rooster weathervane on the garage roof, and we said it had to stay. Her answer was, "Oh I need 100 dollars for that. Well, we gave her a hundred dollars. It was worth it and the rooster is still there in all his glory. Whenever there is a storm, he twists and turns. Surprising he has not fallen off.

We have already been here in New Brunswick for ten years, the longest time we have owned a residence anywhere. Hopefully, we can stay here until we must move to an assisted living or in with one of our girls. I haven't said anything about that to them yet but we are planning to move in with one of them.

In 2014, my Dad called us and asked us to come back to Langley and help them. I was not sure what he was implying but I knew it was probably time to go help my parents with their house and all.

I had a foot care business at that time, and I had to send letters to all the clients to let them know that I was leaving and that they would have to find another nurse. I felt bad about this. We rented our lovely home in Boundary Creek to the realtor that we had purchased it from, packed up most of our so-called precious things and headed across the country with our new little dog, Oscar. The entire process was a matter of 10 days and we had it all organized.

It was a great trip but long. It was wonderful being able to visit again with our cousins in Peterborough as we passed through. When growing up I have the fondest memories of travelling to Peterborough, with my grandparents, for holidays.

When we arrived in BC, we called Mom's from Boston Bar and she said that she would have supper ready. My dear sweet momma had a salmon meal waiting for us. It was so lovely to be there. I really could not believe we made it. We stayed with my folks in their large townhouse, so we were fine there and Mom loved Oscar the dog. Since the passing of my sweet momma, my Dad loves to tell the story, "Oh your mother loved Oscar" and he would go on to say, "He would come into the house and run into the bedroom, jump on my bed and then over to Mom and she would pull the covers down and they would go to sleep". I did actually witness this once or twice. It is a truly lovely memory. We went for 6 weeks and stayed for 6 years.

2008

Prior to making the move to the East Coast, Frank and I made plans to go house hunting. We had sold our house in Western Canada and had enough cash to buy another one in the East where real estate was a fraction of Vancouver's prices. We could afford a house in our retirement years! Prices in the East were definitely more affordable for pensioners. As a result, we could in fact buy another house and make the mortgage payments with our meagre pensions.

2014

"I decided that I wasn't going to just sit around all day. I got in touch with Fraser Health and had an interview for both the Surrey Mental Health and also White Rock Mental Health. Shortly afterwards, I started part-time at White Rock Mental Health and worked three and sometimes four days a week. This was great, and I loved being back at work. Later, I applied to work at Surrey Mental Health in a temporary full-time position and got the job. So, there I was, retired and back to work and I stayed on until I officially retired again from nursing in 2019.

2015

While I was working, I realized that I would need something to do when I retired, so I started to pursue my Master's in Theology. Theology, you say. Well, I had grown up in the church, but I always wanted to know more about what religion was all about and Christianity too. I read the bible but not as much as most. I studied independently and when I finished that, my professor thought I would be a good candidate for a Doctorate in Counselling. So, I finished that too. He believed that private counselling would be a good direction as I had both degrees. I agreed and I really enjoyed the work. That is what I am doing now in retirement. I also created a website as well and called it, "counselling with Susan".

After Mom's passing, we were a little unsure about when to leave BC. It had always been our plan to return to our home in New Brunswick eventually, but the Covid-19 Pandemic presented itself early in 2020 so we decided to return to Boundary Creek that summer. It was so difficult to leave my Dad behind. Minor correction. He did come with us on the across Canada trip but he would only stay a short time. He had to get back to his condo where memories of my mother were still alive for him. Before he returned, however, we did make a few nostalgic visits at his request. One trip was to Jordan Ferry where we buried Mom's ashes in the same spot as her grandparents. That was emotional for Dad but he wanted to do it. We also went to see where his mother had her summer home in Elms dale, Nova Scotia. We drove by the houses we had lived in while living in Halifax and went to my Dad's family house on Chebucto Road. He was incredibly pleased.

We are now getting settled back home. As my friends here say, "You are finally home." It does feel like home but a part of me really misses my friends in the west.

Moving back to New Brunswick was a choice we made, more affordable and quieter. No hustle and bustle of a big city. We really enjoy rural New Brunswick, close enough to the city with only 17 to 20 minutes to the all the big box shops. Not bad. Who says' you can't go back? We came back and we love out little lodge in the woods.

Our house was in fairly good shape, or so we thought until we had been back a little while. One thing after another after another began popping up. It has cost us a fortune to put things back to order. The washing machine needed replacing and my leather sofa and loveseat were destroyed. Who does that?? I was so irritated by the lack of respect the renter had for other people's property. I know it was just a sofa but it cost a lot of money. This was way more than normal wear and tear on a furniture. There were marks and jabs in the walls that had been patched but were still obvious. We will not rent our place again. We will just have some one check on it. Once burnt! Twice shy!! We were thankful to have someone in the place at least. We took a chance and it was alright. I guess we really have to chalk up the things we have to fix to normal wear and tear. We lived through it and were able to help my parents out west. I'm so thankful for the time we spent with Mom and Dad. Nothing can replace that.

2014 -2020

While we were still out in BC, we helped my parents sell their place and totally moved them, packing all their precious things and moving them into their new condo. It was a lot of work. My husband, bless his heart, moved most of it and they were not even his parents. He said, "It's life." We came for six weeks and stayed for six years. We do not begrudge one single moment of it. We enjoyed their company and had so much fun laughing and playing cards, bridge that is. To my Dad, there is no other game. We have so many great memories. No regrets and no feelings of martyrdom at all. I love my parents and will pay it forward. I would do it all again with a smile not expecting anything in return. That is how we should live. Do a good turn for no other reason than it is the right thing to do. This is my belief.

How did we get here from there? That is my biggest question.

The sequence of events in life determines our destiny, our future, and where we will end up. There is a philosophy that believes that there are no mistakes, no errors. Everything happens just as it is supposed to happen. I find that hard to swallow sometimes. We will find ourselves saying "if only this or that". The choices we make and of course, the journey they lead to are always a mystery to me.

I went back to Saint John in 1971 for a wee visit and at that time I thought, "Should I stay or should I return?" Well, everyone knows what happened. I did not stay and I returned to Edmonton and Frank and we picked up where we left off. A while later when my mother-in-law put on a bridal shower for me, there was whispering around the circle of ladies. We always wondered if you would come back. I was a little shocked that this was a topic of conversation amongst these high-class ladies. I had made my trip east because

I was out of a job at the time, so it was the perfect time. Frank, however, had shared with his mom and Dad that he thought I was not coming back. That was the gist of that rumor. I just smiled and nodded and looked lovely as always. I can certainly see how life would have been quite different if I had chosen to stay, quite different indeed.

My dream now is to construct a tiny cottage on our property for us to live in when we get old. I am not too sure when that will be because I do not plan to get old. A dear friend once said to me (she is younger than me), "You are not old till you are dead." The little house will be a granny and grandpa cottage too. We will be back in the trees and the youngsters will be in the log house. I don't think this is an unreasonable dream to have. Maybe a little selfish but it is time to be all about us at that stage.

2019

This was the year my mom died. She was continually saying that she had pain in her right outer thigh. She would say "oh it is not pain, it just feels horrible, and when I rub it, it feels better." We had taken mom to the hospital in February of the year she turned 89 and she had trouble breathing. She said to the doctor, "I just want to make it to 90." Then she would chuckle. Another time when she was having trouble breathing, we went to the hospital again. This was when they found a small spot on her lungs and they felt it was cancer. We took her again in August of 2019 and learned that she had had a small stroke this time. She did not stay in the hospital over night, but she was never the same after that. I think she had a few little mini strokes as well. As time went on, her lungs would fill up and she had difficulty breathing.

About four weeks before she passed away, Jessica was wondering if she should come for a visit from India. She so loved her grandmother. I told her that if she wanted to see her again, she better come right away. She arrived September 12 and stayed with Mom and Dad to give Dad a hand with Mom. It was truly a blessing.

Mom was gone the 22 September. Kaitlyn, my niece, came over for the last couple of nights. The two granddaughters were close by when she needed something extra those last two nights. Grandma was quite lucid to the end. She said she wanted something to eat and said "A donut please." So, Jess headed over to Tim Horton's and fulfilled her wish. Dad didn't want Mom to go into hospice, so we chose to keep her at home and the hospice nurses came to the condominium. Jessica and I administered the pain medication. We were all there when mom took her last breath. I was making supper for us all when she passed. I still recall my sister-in-law coming down the hall toward the kitchen asking me to check and see if she had really gone. We were all there around the bed. It was so precious to be there when she died. I loved my mom and so miss her.it may seem a little sacrilegious doing what we did but we poured a bottle of white wine and we all stood around mom's bed and said a farewell and toasted the lovely lady that she was. trip was to Jordan Ferry where we buried Mom's ashes in the same spot as her grandparents. That was emotional for Dad, but he wanted to do it. We also went to see where his mother had her summer home in Elms dale, Nova Scotia. We drove by the houses we had lived while living in Halifax and went to my Dad's family house on Chebucto Road. He was incredibly pleased. Dad decided to return home where he could visit mom in the memory garden at St. George's Anglican church in Fort Langley. So, we drove him to Halifax airport, and he took a flight to Toronto where my brother Colin and my nephew Nicholas met him. It was sad to see him go but he was so restless still.

Then came my Dad's long and painful grieving. He has had an exceedingly difficult time living once my mom passed away. She had been gone about 8 months and he was still crying every day. It has been incredibly sad and difficult to witness. I have been sad sometimes too, wondering who needed anti-depressants, me or my Dad. He probably will never ever get over her loss. He keeps repeating "Why didn't she tell us?" I try to comfort him and say she did not know either. But there is some decline in his thinking processes, so he keeps ruminating over these thoughts which makes it extremely difficult for him.

It has been especially hard since we returned to the east coast. He has found solace in the neighbours. they helped him turn on his washer and he gets his clothes washed sometime. Dad does need someone anyone living with him, but Dad gets so lonely, doesn't eat, and has lost an incredible amount of weight. Colin's wife very kindly has sent meals to Dad but he wasn't eating them all the time. He felt some guilt but he usually preferred to go across the street to Denny's so he wouldn't be alone. It is just too hard to eat on your own. the local Denny's across the street has become a regular haunt. . The staff run circles around him when he arrives, and he loves the attention. Who would not love it? Thankfully our prayers have been answered my daughter who was living in India had returned and she and her wonderful husband Danny are living with him. It is working out really great for everyone.

Dad wanted us to try to get along, this is all very sad for dad that the four of us can not socialize. We are all so different and have different life expectations.

The Last Chapter

I have led a very prosperous and exciting life. I have experienced many things throughout my life, and I have a love for helping those in need. When I was in training, some of my classmates thought that most people who go into the psychiatric field have some of their own issues and that they hope to find the solution while they were working in the field.

This was not the case for me. I am not saying that I did not have any issues. We all know that everyone has issues, but I did not have a mental illness. My sister-in-law probably would disagree. My daughter (do not remember which one now) said I know this couple and they are the perfect couple, never fight and they are perfect. Well, that is not quite accurate. We have other friends too we visited many times and they always presented as the perfect couple. We dropped in on them one day. Well, their house was a mess, and they too were having a little argument, or let's say a disagreement as well. And Rosie looked at us and said" Yes Susan even us!" and I said "No one is perfect."

There was, and is, some history of mental illness in my family though, so I knew a great deal about the illness and how it affects families and not in a positive way either. There is a lot of prejudice toward those with mental illness. A lot of this comes from fear and misunderstanding. I have a cousin who has schizophrenia, and her husband had a cousin who also had schizophrenia. It is in everyone's family. No one is exempt. Frank had a cousin who had schizophrenia and unfortunately, she took her life.

I recall a patient when I was working on the Psychiatric Unit at Moncton city Hospital, who, when I asked him, "How are you doing Jason?" He replied, "Living the Dream". Several years have passed and I am now retired from nursing. When people ask "How are you doing," I often reply, "I'm living the dream."

How much of my past do I tell? What should I keep to my self and how much do I lay on the table and tell the world? I may feel the backlash of friends, both close friends and not so close.

I like this quote by Virginia Satir

> *Life is not what it is supposed to be. It is what it is. The way you cope with it is what makes the difference.*

And I may have painted my husband in a little bit of a negative light, (So sorry Frank, I do love you). And all in all, he is a pretty great guy. He usually is late for supper but other than that … oh yes, he forgot my birthday many times and our anniversary too. He is getting better. But I say he is kind and loyal and he does the housework. I cannot believe that any partner would turn that down for a lifelong relationship. I have seen that poster that says, "Stamp out housework" and I am in total agreement with that statement. My girls think he is the bees' knees and I have already mentioned someone else about when I was working at the dry cleaners. Their papa could do no wrong in their eyes. That is good. There are many fathers out there that need a crash course in what to do or need to be shown the job description.

I started out with selling sunglasses and ended up with a Ph.D. in Counselling. Go figure, eh! That is grammatically incorrect, but I had to say "eh" since I am truly a Canadian.

I will end this by saying that this is not the last of my writing. There are many bits missing, but I wanted to share with you the bulk of my life happenings.

As a woman I did not speak up enough. My husband would disagree profusely, but I did talk but never felt I was heard, especially in the company of men. So, I say, "Ladies, speak up!" "Let your voices be heard!" We have a lot to say and most of it is vital to humanity!!!

Add to that, "Don't ever give up on your dreams or, for that matter, your goals. Make a difference in the life of someone else. Pay it forward as someone once said. I will leave you on a positive note. "Love one another and always be kind." I know this may sound corny but truer words have never been spoken.

I feel I have just brushed the tip of the iceberg here with this brief overview of my travels. I have so much more to tell to fill in the blanks. I have been so many places and done so many things that I really believe that I have earned the title of "Gypsy Sue". I have been very stable in my life but having said that, I have to admit that I have moved to many different geographic places over my lifetime for many valid reasons. Cheer!!

High school grad picture

me and my brother Colin

Group photo of the Cuddlies Gang in the store.

Our business card for Cuddlies and Co.

Mom and I on my wedding day

Me and Dorothy when she came to Edmonton for my wedding.

Me with Karen and Jessica in Viking 1977

My girls with my grandparents Ella and Oscar
on their 60th wedding anniversary.

Me Frank Tracy and Karen and her friend Tracy in Fort smith 1983

Favorite picture of Jessica and Karen

My wonderful parents Marg and Tom Taylor

Two high school friends—Marg and Marcia

Ann and Susan—2013

Epilogue

I have been writing this memoir for over 10 years and when I read other people's memoirs, I think "wow" what they have accomplished in their lives. My life seems quite pale by comparison. Then there will be others who read this and say oh my gosh look at what she has done and look how she treats people. I know my life has been interesting!

I have just barely scraped the tip of the iceberg when it comes to my story but I have laid out a framework of who I am and what I have become.

I owe a lot to my parents who were always there for me through thick and thin. They have been so supportive of me all my life. Sometimes I wish they had pushed me more and I would have been a more out of the box thinker but they did have a big impact on my moving forward and their lifestyle has been a strong influence on me. I always wanted to please my parents and even to the point of going into nursing the first time and foregoing teachers' college. That has got to be my one true regret in life. As it turns out I had a remarkably interesting career as a nurse, so it did not turn out all that bad.

Several years before my mom passed away, I started to work on my doctorate in counselling. I managed to complete it before she passed, so my other goal in my journey, is to have a private practice. I also believe you are never too old to change your path. I like to think I will be still writing or counselling until I am 92 or more, just like Dr. Ruth Wetheimier, the famous sex therapist.

Before I go any further with this last chapter, I want to thank all those who helped me in the writing of the book

I do know that all failures are not bad and they make us who we are. Life is not meant to be a smooth ride. Nothing comes without a challenge.

Firstly, I want to thank Leslie PRYCE-Jones Childs who has done my editing for me. She has been an amazing coach. I hope she will be there for the next book. Leslie, you do have a way with words.

Secondly, I want to show my appreciation and gratitude to Sandra Crawford for writing an introduction to the book. You are a true friend indeed.

And lastly but not least, I would like to thank my artist friend, Sharon Green. She is my other best friend, and has done the drawings in the book.

You may ask where do I go from here? This is not the end of my journey and I plan to continue to write and will fill in all the blanks that have been omitted in this episode.

I live ever cautiously by my subtitle "Life is not a dress rehearsal". Keep a watchful eye for my next book to be published soon.

> In all your ways acknowledge him, and he will make your paths straight.
>
> Prov.3:6

TO BE CONTINUED

CPSIA information can be obtained
at www.ICGtesting.com
Printed in the USA
BVHW032259280521
608406BV00001BA/3

9 781982 268640